THIS PAGE:
Winsor Castle was constructed in the early 1870s to
protect the water supply flowing from springs—
collectively referred to as "Pipe Spring"—associated
with the underlying Sevier Fault.

ON THE COVER:
Red rocks of the Jurassic Kayenta Formation
comprise much of the slopes to the west of the fort.
Lighter-colored rocks of the Jurassic Navajo
Sandstone cap the ridges.

National Park Service photographs courtesy Andrea
Bornemeier (Pipe Spring NM).

Pipe Spring National Monument
Geologic Resources Inventory Report

Natural Resource Report NPS/NRPC/GRD/NRR—2009/164

Geologic Resources Division
Natural Resource Program Center
P.O. Box 25287
Denver, Colorado 80225

January 2010

U.S. Department of the Interior
National Park Service
Natural Resource Program Center
Denver, Colorado

The National Park Service, Natural Resource Program Center publishes a range of reports that address natural resource topics of interest and applicability to a broad audience in the National Park Service and others in natural resource management, including scientists, conservation and environmental constituencies, and the public.

The Natural Resource Report Series is used to disseminate high-priority, current natural resource management information with managerial application. The series targets a general, diverse audience, and may contain NPS policy considerations or address sensitive issues of management applicability.

All manuscripts in the series receive the appropriate level of peer review to ensure that the information is scientifically credible, technically accurate, appropriately written for the intended audience, and designed and published in a professional manner. This report received informal peer review by subject-matter experts who were not directly involved in the collection, analysis, or reporting of the data.

Views, statements, findings, conclusions, recommendations, and data in this report are those of the author(s) and do not necessarily reflect views and policies of the National Park Service, U.S. Department of the Interior. Mention of trade names or commercial products does not constitute endorsement or recommendation for use by the National Park Service.

Printed copies of this report are produced in a limited quantity and they are only available as long as the supply lasts. This report is available from the Geologic Resources Inventory website (http://www.nature.nps.gov/geology/inventory/gre_publications.cfm) and the Natural Resource Publications Management website (http://www.nature.nps.gov/publications/ NRPM).

Please cite this publication as:

Graham, J. 2010. Pipe Spring National Monument Geologic Resources Inventory Report. Natural Resource Report NPS/NRPC/GRD/NRR—2009/164. National Park Service, Denver, Colorado.

NPS 321/100624, January 2010

Contents

List of Figures

Executive Summary

This report accompanies the digital geologic map for Pipe Spring National Monument in Arizona, which the Geologic Resources Division produced in collaboration with its partners. It contains information relevant to resource management and scientific research. This document incorporates preexisting geologic information and does not include new data or additional fieldwork.

Established in 1923, Pipe Spring National Monument is a memorial to pioneer life and protects the springs that were so critical to both American Indians and 19th century pioneers who settled in the arid climate of northwestern Arizona. The four springs that are known collectively as "Pipe Spring" include Main Spring, Spring Room Spring, Tunnel Spring, and West Cabin Spring. The monument's 16 hectares (40 acres) are located in the Arizona Strip, a geographical area north of the Grand Canyon and south of Utah's southern border.

The high plateaus that are bounded by steep cliffs in this part of northwestern Arizona and southwestern Utah are part of the western margin of the larger Colorado Plateau geologic province. Relatively flat-lying sedimentary rock layers (strata) in this part of the Colorado Plateau have been deformed into broad folds. The sedimentary rocks at Pipe Spring National Monument consist of Triassic and Jurassic strata, composed primarily of siltstone and sandstone. Slopes composed of the more easily eroded siltstone form slope aprons at the base of the sandstone cliffs.

The north-south trending Sevier Fault is the primary structural feature in Pipe Spring National Monument. Strata on the west side of the fault have been moved downward relative to the rocks on the east side of the fault, so that porous and fractured Navajo Sandstone, the rock unit containing the principal groundwater aquifer in the region, lies adjacent to impermeable siltstone and claystone of the older Moenkopi Formation. The sandstone has been folded into a trough, called a "syncline," which parallels the Sevier Fault and acts as a conduit and temporary holding pond for groundwater flow.

Sustaining groundwater flow to the springs is the most important geologic issue at Pipe Spring National Monument. In 1971, the National Park Service (NPS) drilled a well along the Sevier Fault to supply drinking water to the monument. Following completion of the NPS well, groundwater flow to the springs began to decrease. In 1975, the Kaibab-Paiute Tribe drilled a well to supply water to Kaibab Village, further decreasing groundwater flow to the springs. Today, total spring flow comes primarily from Tunnel Spring. Main Spring and Spring Room Spring are dry, and the flow from West Cabin Spring is negligible.

Groundwater pumping is the primary cause of spring flow decline at Pipe Spring National Monument. If pumping stops, spring flow should increase. Research is being conducted to study the fracture zones, recharge areas, and groundwater pathways associated with the springs at Pipe Spring National Monument. Alternative well sites to supply water to buildings at the monument and to Kaibab are under consideration.

Potential seismic (earthquake) hazards also pose a significant geologic issue. Ground shaking may influence groundwater flow and damage the springs. In addition, Winsor Castle straddles the Sevier Fault. Most of the 400 m (1,300 ft) of displacement along the Sevier Fault occurred between 10,000 years and 5.3 million years ago, but tectonic activity continues in the region. Indeed, estimates range from 0.07 to 0.18 millimeters per year for displacement rates on the Arizona portion of the Sevier Fault. In this area, large earthquakes with magnitudes of 6.5 to 7.5 on the Richter scale occur infrequently, approximately every 5,000 to 30,000 years. However, the age of the last large earthquake to impact Pipe Spring National Monument is unknown.

A secondary issue at Pipe Spring National Monument involves the preservation of dinosaur tracks that were discovered in 1988. The footprints were made by an unidentified bipedal carnivorous dinosaur.

The springs are relatively recent features at this location, but the colorful bands of strata in the Pipe Spring vicinity record a geologic history extending back in time to the Permian Period, about 270 million years ago. A variety of marine and non-marine depositional environments inundated northwestern Arizona in the geologic past. Shallow marine limestone and sandstone of the Permian gave way to near-shore, mudflat, floodplain, and river environments in the Triassic Period. Evidence of these past environments includes ripple marks, mudcracks, algal features, and thin layers of gypsum. During the Jurassic, sand dunes covered vast areas of Utah and Arizona. During the Cretaceous Period, an incursion by an inland sea that extended from the Arctic to the Gulf of Mexico flooded this arid environment, and inundated the western interior of North America.

In the Late Cretaceous-middle Tertiary, approximately 70 to 35 million years ago, lithospheric plate collisions along the western active margin of North America caused the Rocky Mountains to form and drained the inland sea from the continent. Compressive west-to-east tectonic forces displaced great tracts of continental crust, thrusting deeply buried older rocks to the surface and over younger strata. During this mountain building episode, called the Laramide Orogeny, the relatively horizontal strata near Pipe Spring were folded into the geologic feature known as the Moccasin monocline.

In the Miocene Epoch, about 15 million years ago, extensional forces began to pull apart the crust, forming today's Basin-and-Range physiographic province, a geologic region that includes parts of the southwestern United States and northwestern Mexico. North-south trending mountain ranges separated by structural basins with very little relief characterize today's Basin-and-Range topography. The east–west extensional stresses, which continue today, impacted the western margin of the Colorado Plateau, and reactivated the Sevier Fault, a remnant of an earlier Cretaceous mountain building episode.

Periods of uplift and erosion over the last 65 million years have developed today's landscape of high plateaus

and steep-walled canyons that characterize the Colorado Plateau. Landslides are common along the Vermilion Cliffs and other steep escarpments that mark the borders of the plateaus. Alluvial deposits fan out at the bases of cliffs where canyons discharge sediment. In this dry climate, wind transports fine sand eroded from the ancient sand dunes of Navajo Sandstone. Amid this relatively harsh environment, the springs at Pipe Spring National Monument provided an oasis for the early settlers in northwestern Arizona. The springs, Winsor Castle, the old Whitmore-McInytre dugout, stone walls and other historic markers preserve a hint of what life was like during the pioneer days on the Arizona Strip.

The glossary on page 41 contains explanations of many technical terms used in this report, including terms used in the Map Unit Properties Table.]

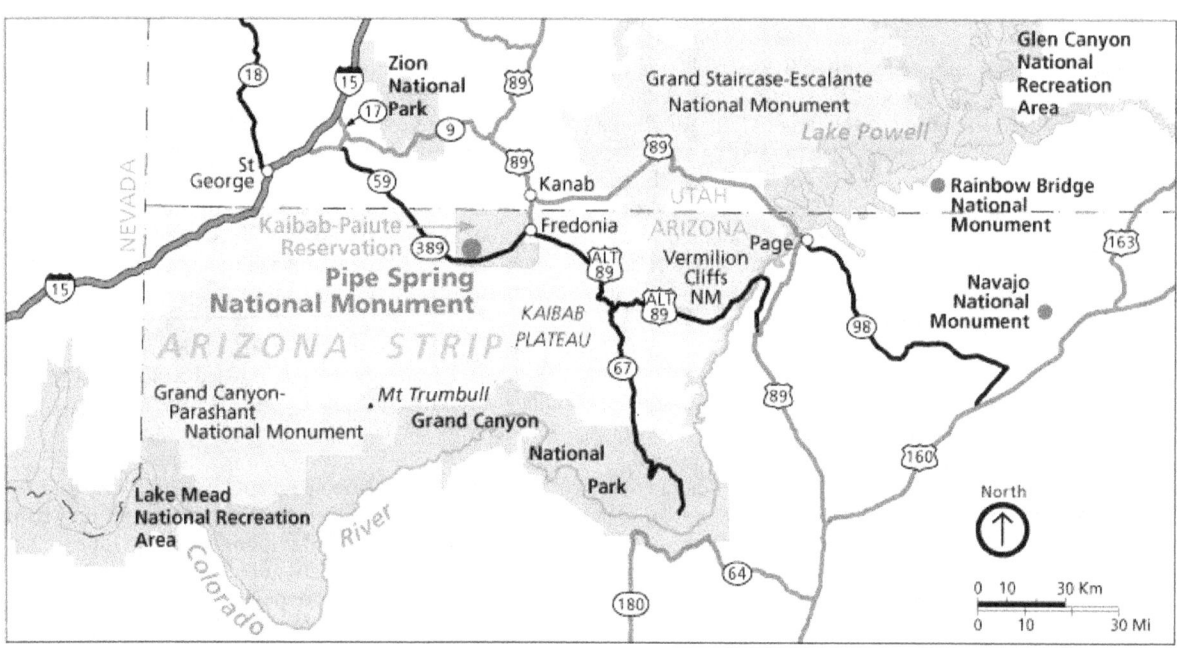

Figure 1. Location map of Pipe Spring National Monument and the Arizona Strip in northwestern Arizona. National Park Service map.

Introduction

The following section briefly describes the National Park Service Geologic Resources Inventory and the regional geologic setting of Pipe Spring National Monument.

Purpose of the Geologic Resources Inventory Program

The Geologic Resources Inventory (GRI) is one of 12 inventories funded under the National Park Service (NPS) Natural Resource Challenge designed to enhance baseline information available to park managers. The program carries out the geologic component of the inventory effort. The Geologic Resources Division of the Natural Resource Program Center administers this program. The GRI team relies heavily on partnerships with the U.S. Geological Survey, Colorado State University, state surveys, and others in developing GRI products.

The goal of the GRI is to increase understanding of the geologic processes at work in parks and provide sound geologic information for use in park decision making. Sound park stewardship relies on understanding natural resources and their role in the ecosystem. Geology is the foundation of park ecosystems. The compilation and use of natural resource information by park managers is called for in section 204 of the National Parks Omnibus Management Act of 1998 and in NPS-75, Natural Resources Inventory and Monitoring Guideline.

To realize this goal, the GRI team is systematically conducting a scoping meeting for each of the identified 270 natural area parks and providing a park-specific digital geologic map and geologic report. These products support the stewardship of park resources and are designed for nongeoscientists. Scoping meetings bring together park staff and geologic experts to review available geologic maps and discuss specific geologic issues, features, and processes.

The GRI mapping team converts the geologic maps identified for park use at the scoping meeting into digital geologic data in accordance with their Geographic Information Systems (GIS) Data Model. These digital data sets bring an interactive dimension to traditional paper maps by providing geologic data for use in park GIS and facilitating the incorporation of geologic considerations into a wide range of resource management applications. The newest maps come complete with interactive help files. This geologic report aids in the use of the map and provides park managers with an overview of park geology and geologic resource management issues.

For additional information regarding the content of this report and current GRI contact information please refer to the Geologic Resources Inventory Web site (http://www.nature.nps.gov/geology/inventory/).

Regional Location and Landscape

Pipe Spring National Monument is located south of Zion National Park and north of the Grand Canyon, in a geographical area known as the Arizona Strip (fig. 1). The monument, about 24 km (15 mi) west of Fredonia, Arizona, lies entirely within the Kaibab-Paiute Indian Reservation. Arizona State Highway 389 provides access to the monument's 16 ha (40 ac).

The monument lies at the base of the Vermillion Cliffs escarpment, where Moccasin Terrace tapers to Winsor Point, the southernmost extent of the Vermilion Cliffs (fig. 2). Main Spring, Spring Room Spring, Tunnel Spring, and West Cabin Spring, the four springs known collectively as Pipe Spring, discharge at the base of Winsor Point (fig. 3).

Both the Vermillion Cliffs and Moccasin Terrace are part of the larger Uinkaret Plateau (fig. 4). The Arizona Strip, Uinkaret Plateau, Vermillion Cliffs, and Pipe Spring National Monument all lie within the Colorado Plateau Province, a roughly circular region bordered by the Rocky Mountains to the north and east, and the Basin-and-Range Province to the west and south (fig. 5). High plateaus and isolated mountains characterize the Colorado Plateau, which includes large parts of Arizona, Utah, Colorado, and New Mexico. The Colorado River, for which the plateau was named, drains at least 90% of the plateau.

Approximately 15 million years ago, plate tectonic interactions along the southwestern margin of North America generated east-west extensional stresses. These stresses began to extend or pull apart the crust beneath the Great Basin, initiating what would develop into today's distinctive Basin-and-Range topography of fault-bounded, narrow, north-south trending mountain ranges and basins (fig. 5). Crustal stretching did not extensively deform the Colorado Plateau, but it did leave its mark along the western margin of the province where normal faults cut deeply into the crust. The faults tilt, or dip, steeply at the surface (50-60°) and gradually flatten at great depth. They are considered to be "normal" faults because the rocks in the "hanging wall" above the fault plane have moved downward relative to strata in the "footwall" below the fault plane (fig. 6).

The regionally-extensive Sevier Fault bisects Pipe Spring National Monument and forms the eastern boundary of the Uinkaret Plateau (fig. 4). Strata have been displaced as much as 400 m (1,300 ft) along the Sevier Fault near Pipe Spring (Billingsley et al. 2004).

Deformation of the relatively flat strata on the Colorado Plateau also produced symmetrical convex and concave folds (anticlines and synclines, respectively) and asymmetrical monoclines. Unlike relatively symmetrical anticlines and synclines, monoclines have one gently-dipping limb and one limb that dips more steeply (fig. 7). Monoclines, like Moccasin Monocline in the Pipe Spring area, are prominent features on the Colorado Plateau.

Nearly all of the Colorado Plateau is above 1,500 m (5,000 ft). Elevations at Pipe Spring National Monument range from 1,501 m (4,923 ft) to 1,554 m (5,100 ft). Precipitation in this semiarid climate averages 30 cm/year (12 in/year) and occurs mostly as rainfall (Truini 1999). Sixty percent of the precipitation occurs during the winter. Wet seasons occur during the late winter and spring, and again with the summer monsoon that begins in July and ends in September. A distinct dry season occurs in late spring and early summer, and a less-pronounced drying occurs in the fall. High year-to-year variability is normal. On the Arizona Strip, elevations below 1,500 m (5,000 ft) generally support a sparse growth of sagebrush, cactus, grass, and various high-desert shrubs (Billingsley et al. 2004).

Local Geologic Setting

Stratigraphy

About 198 m (650 ft) of Permian rock and about 1,036 m (3,400 ft) of Triassic and Jurassic strata comprise the sedimentary section in the Pipe Spring National Monument region. Throughout the Arizona Strip, nearly flat-lying Paleozoic and Mesozoic sedimentary layers dip to the north-northeast at about 1-2° and are gently warped by minor north-south-trending folds.

Lower Triassic members of the Moenkopi Formation are the oldest units to crop out in or near Pipe Spring National Monument (fig. 8). Red siltstone and sandstone, gray gypsum, and gray dolomite constitute the relatively impermeable Triassic Moenkopi Formation. A small cliff of white sandstone, the Shinarump Member of the Chinle Formation, overlies the red slopes of the Moenkopi Formation. The Shinarump cliff is overlain by multicolored green and blue mudstones of the Petrified Forest Member of the Chinle Formation.

The lower slopes of the Vermilion Cliffs expose the red-brown claystone, siltstone, and sandstone of the Jurassic Moenave and Kayenta Formations. The light red and white, cross-bedded Jurassic Navajo Sandstone forms towering cliffs in the region, but is present here only as a thin, light-colored cap on the Vermillion Cliffs. Thicker outcrops of Navajo Sandstone comprise the highlands of Moccasin and Moquith Mountains to the north. Regional unconformities that represent gaps in geologic time separate the Triassic strata from the Jurassic strata, and the Jurassic strata from overlying Quaternary deposits.

On most of the Colorado Plateau, the transition between the Kayenta Formation and Navajo Sandstone is clearly defined where the red deposits of Kayenta rivers are overlain by the lighter-colored Navajo sand dunes. The transition is complicated in the Pipe Spring National

Monument area, however, because rivers returned after the initial influx of dune sand. As a result, a thin unit of fluvial deposits called the "Tenney Canyon Tongue" of the Kayenta Formation and a thin sand dune unit called the "Lamb Point Tongue" of the Navajo Sandstone separate the main body of Navajo Sandstone from the main body of the Kayenta Formation (fig. 8). The Lamb Point Tongue is mapped just west of the park while the Tenney Canyon Tongue is mapped about 7 km (4.4 mi) north of the park (Billingsley et al. 2004). The interpretation of the Navajo Sandstone in the northwest corner of the monument by Billingsley and others (2004) as the main body of the Navajo Sandstone (Jn) is preferred over the description in Sharrow (2009) as the Lamb Point tongue (Jnl) (Dave Sharrow, hydrologist, National Park Service, written communication, February 1, 2010).

Quaternary sediments are widely distributed throughout the region and consist of unconsolidated gravel, sand, and finer-grained material that form fluvial deposits, alluvial fans, eolian sand sheets, and sand dunes. The steep, southwestward-facing escarpment of the Vermilion Cliffs generate rock talus and landslide deposits. The only Quaternary deposits mapped within the monument comprise alluvial fan and stream deposits of silt, sand, and gravel that spread out from the base of the Vermilion Cliffs (Billingsley et al. 2004).

Structure

At Pipe Spring, the Sevier Fault and Moccasin Monocline disrupt the sinuous east-west trend of the Vermillion Cliffs. The Sevier Fault, which forms the principal structural feature at Pipe Springs National Monument, has offset, or moved, the cliffs east of the fault 14 km (9 mi) to the north, leaving Winsor Point and the monument as relatively high ground projecting into the Arizona Strip (fig. 4).

The intersection of the Sevier Fault with the ground surface can be traced for over 160 km (100 mi) to the north and south. A short segment of the Sevier Fault branches to the west from the main fault trace about 1.6 km (1 mi) north of Pipe Spring National Monument (Billingsley et al. 2004). Approximately 21 km (13 mi) south of the monument, the Sevier Fault acquires a slightly southwest – northeast trend and connects to the Toroweap Fault, which crosses the Grand Canyon.

Folding of the normally flat-lying strata formed the east-dipping Moccasin Monocline and elevated the landscape about 60-90 m (200-300 ft) west of the Sevier Fault. Strata on the over-steepened limb of the Moccasin Monocline dip east as much as 10° towards the fault. A concave, trough-shaped syncline at the base of the Moccasin Monocline parallels the trend of the west segment of the Sevier Fault (fig. 9). Fractured Navajo Sandstone within the syncline acts as a conduit for groundwater flow to Pipe Spring.

The west segment of the Sevier Fault, Moccasin Monocline, and associated syncline can be followed to the northwest until they reach Moccasin Mountain about 3.2 km (2 mi) north of Moccasin, Arizona. Farther to the north, recent geophysical studies have found several joints or faults with small displacements that extend back to the northeast and rejoin the main Sevier Fault in the vicinity of Coral Pink Sand Dunes State Park in Utah (Mayerle and Urquhart 2008). Quaternary fluvial and eolian (wind) deposits obscure the Sevier Fault south of Pipe Spring National Monument (Billingsley et al. 2004).

Springs in the Region

Springs in the Pipe Spring area owe their existence to fractures associated with the Sevier Fault, joints in the bedrock, the juxtaposition across the Sevier Fault of impermeable strata against permeable sandstone, and the syncline at the base of Moccasin Monocline. Joints and fractures in the rock act as conduits for groundwater flow, while the porous and permeable Navajo Sandstone acts as a reservoir that accumulates and stores groundwater. The impermeable mudstones and siltstones of the Kayenta Formation, which underlie the Navajo Sandstone, act as a barrier to the downward percolation of groundwater, while the abundant claystone and gypsum in the Chinle and Moenkopi Formations prevent lateral groundwater leakage eastward across the Sevier Fault. North of the monument, the syncline of fractured Navajo Sandstone acts as a conduit to transport groundwater from north to south along the Sevier Fault zone (Billingsley et al. 2004; Martin 2007).

Springs associated with the contact between the Navajo Sandstone and Kayenta Formation include Pipe Spring, Moccasin Spring, Upper Moccasin Springs, Red Cliffs Spring (Moquith Mountains), Bull Pasture Spring, Meeks Spring (in upper Potter Canyon), and an unnamed spring in Rosy Canyon, northwest of Meeks Spring (fig. 10). Some springs, such as Pipe Spring, Moccasin Spring, and the small cluster of springs known as Upper Moccasin Springs, are known to have discharges greater than 4 liters per minute (lpm) [>1 gallon per minute (gpm)], while the other springs and seeps in the area have relatively small discharges, generally less than 4 lpm (<1 gpm) (Billingsley et al. 2004).

Cultural History

A memorial to pioneer life, Pipe Spring National Monument contains a rich and storied past. Throughout the centuries, spring water has proved critical to survival on the Arizona Strip. Archeological evidence indicates that springs in the monument have attracted people to the site for the past 8,000 years (Truini et al. 2004).

Ceramic shards, charcoal deposits, and structural remains from the Virgin/Kayenta Ancestral Puebloan people (often called "Anasazi") (approximately 1100-1150 C.E. [Common Era]) are found in all portions of the monument, along with petroglyphs (called "Tumpee'po'-ohp" by the Kaibab Paiute) and pictographs (fig. 11) (McKoy 2000). These early inhabitants, known as the E'nengweng (Old Ones, also spelled "Tinung wung") to the Paiutes, Hisatsinom to the Hopi, and Anasazi to the Navajo, built permanent pueblos and pithouses near

Matungwa'va (Yellow Dripping Rock), the spring later known as Pipe Spring. They used water from the spring to grow corn, beans and squash.

One of a number of distinct Southern Paiute bands that have inhabited the Arizona Strip, the Kaibab Paiute (Kai'vi'vits) believe this area to be their ancestral home. A conservative estimate of their traditional territory includes 12,494 sq km (4,824 sq mi) (McKoy 2000).

Early Spanish explorers and later Euro-Americans interacted with the Southern Paiute from 1776 to 1847. The first historical reference to the native peoples comes from two Franciscan priests, Francisco A. Dominguez and Silvestre Velez de Escalante, who led an expedition through northern parts of the Southern Paiute territory in 1776. Fur trappers such as Jedediah Smith, William Wolfskill, and Ewing Young followed the 1776 expedition in the early 1800s. Large numbers of prospectors and pioneers journeyed through Southern Paiute territory after gold was discovered in California in 1849.

Slavery played a significant role in the lives of the Southern Paiute prior to the arrival of Mormon pioneers. By the early 1600s, slavery was common in the Spanish colonies of northern New Mexico and southern California. Ute and Navajo slave raiders, American trappers, and Spanish expeditions all enslaved Southern Paiutes. McKoy (2000) reports that, prior to 1860, nearly one-half of Paiute children were slaves.

On October 30, 1858, Chief Naraguts, a Kaibab Paiute, guided Jacob Hamblin, an emissary of the Mormon Church, and his party of pioneers across the Utah border and into the Arizona Strip. They camped one night at Matungwa'va spring. According to one story, in order to prove his claim as an excellent marksman, William Hamblin, Jacob's brother, took a pipe and set it on a rock. He moved back fifty paces, and hit the pipe with one shot. From then on, the spring was known to Anglo Americans as "Pipe Spring" (Bagley 2002).

Hamblin's stories of abundant grasslands and scattered springs across the Arizona Strip encouraged Mormons to settle there. Soon thousands of cattle and sheep grazed on the Arizona Strip. The settlers and their cattle required a consistent, stable source of water. Pipe Spring became one of those sources. By 1860 the spring was a common water hole and campsite for ranchers.

Mormon expansion moved quickly. Settlers occupied the richest river valleys, reduced the game, and claimed the grassland and water holes as their own. In this arid land, control of the water meant control of all commerce. The Mormons' concept of land ownership and livestock led to conflicts with the Indians. For example, Indians could not understand why Mormons could hunt deer, but they could not hunt cattle. Chief Black Hawk began leading Ute raids against Mormon settlements. Refusing to leave northern Arizona for a reservation in New Mexico, the famous Navajo warrior, Manuelito, and other Navajos joined Chief Black Hawk.

In 1863, James M. Whitmore, a Texas convert to Mormonism, received a land certificate for 65 ha (160 ac) around Pipe Spring. He built a dugout shelter and proceeded to raise longhorn cattle, sheep, grape vines, and fruit trees. Although its roof collapsed years ago, the dugout's remains can still be viewed today northeast of Winsor Castle (fig. 3).

During this time, conflicts between the Indians and settlers intensified, primarily over the 'theft' of settlers' livestock. In January 1866, a band of Navajos drove off the cattle at Pipe Spring. Whitmore and his ranch hand, Robert McIntyre, went to investigate and never returned. Two Indians, captured while hunting cattle, led a group of Mormon militiamen to the bodies of Whitmore and McIntyre. The Mormon militia retaliated and executed a number of Paiute men who Jacob Hamblin later learned had been innocent (McKoy 2000).

This incident stirred further violence, and on April 7, 1866, settlers Joseph Berry, Robert Berry, and his wife Isabella were killed by Indians at the location now known as Berry Knolls, about 2.4 km (1.5 mi) south of Colorado City (McKoy 2000). The mounting danger to the Mormon settlers caused Brigham Young to declare martial law, and to urge the abandonment of small frontier settlements. He advised that all settlements should have a minimum of 150 well-armed men (McKoy 2000).

Upon Whitmore's death, Brigham Young bought the Pipe Spring deed from Whitmore's widow. Young wanted to use the Whitmore ranch to house a tithing herd in the southern part of the state. Tithing, which amounted to a tenth of a church member's income, was sometimes paid with cattle, and Pipe Spring became an excellent place to keep the donated cattle.

In April 1870, Young decided that a fort should be constructed on the side (McKoy 2000). Fort Arizona, as the fort was originally named, was designed to protect the water supply as well as the settlers in the event of an Indian attack.

Fort Arizona consisted of two rectangular stone buildings, with stone walls connecting them to form a courtyard. Channelized spring water flowed through the fort. John Wesley Powell, who obtained supplies at Pipe Spring for his 1871 and 1872 Grand Canyon expeditions, renamed the fort "Winsor Castle" in honor of the fort's first manager Anson P. Winsor. The castle was completed by the early part of 1872.

At about the same time that the fort was being constructed, the Deseret Telegraph Company was stringing a telegraph line from Rockville, Utah, to Kanab, Utah. The telegraph reached St. George, Utah, on January 15, 1867 and was then extended to Pipe Spring. Thus, Pipe Spring became the first telegraph station in Arizona. The arrival of the telegraph ended the isolation of these remote settlements, allowing the pioneers to communicate with the outside world.

Winsor Castle was never attacked. The nearby Kaibab Paiute were friendly, and on November 15, 1870, Jacob Hamblin and Major John Wesley Powell negotiated a peace treaty with the Navajo at Fort Defiance in Arizona. After the treaty was signed, the Navajo stopped raiding white settlements. However, they continued raiding Southern Paiute settlements, eventually causing the Paiutes to seek refuge with other American Indian groups, such as the Hualapai and Havasupai. Some Paiute moved to more isolated places in the lower Kanab Creek area, or along the Colorado River in the Grand Canyon (McKoy 2000).

By 1879 the tithing herd had grown to 2,269 head of cattle and 162 horses. Products such as butter, cheese and beef were sold at the fort. The route through Pipe Spring became part of the "Honeymoon Trail," as visitors from settlements farther south and east stopped at Winsor Castle on their way to get married at the Mormon temple in St. George.

In 1888, the federal government threatened to confiscate church lands because of the Mormon Church's practice of polygamy. The church decided to sell the fort to D.F. Saunders, a non-Mormon cattleman. Pipe Spring was sold several times before becoming a national monument by proclamation No. 1663 on May 31, 1923 (NPS 2004).

The springs, so critical to sustaining pioneer life, were one reason Pipe Spring was established as a monument (NPS 2004). Today, the primary historic resources at the monument include the Pipe Spring fort, the east cabin, the west cabin, and the historic-period sites of the Whitmore-McInytre dugout and a lime kiln (McKoy 2000). The site also includes stone walls, the quarry trail, and the fort ponds (figs. 3 and 18). A vegetable garden, orchard, vineyard, telegraph line, and corrals have been restored.

Figure 2. Winsor Point and Pipe Spring National Monument, as viewed from south of the monument. Winsor Point is the southernmost extent of the Vermillion Cliffs. Sedimentary strata include the Jurassic Navajo Sandstone (Jn) and the Kayenta Formation (Jk). The dotted line represents the approximate contact between the Quaternary valley surface deposits of young alluvial fan material (Qa1) and mixed eolian and fluvial sediments (Qae). Modified from a photograph by Dave Sharrow, hydrologist, National Park Service.

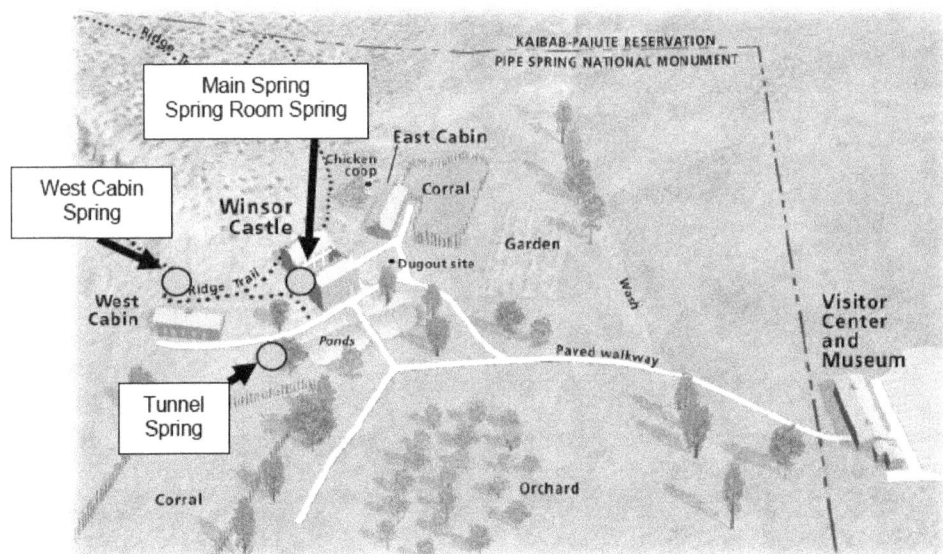

Figure 3. Location of the four springs at Pipe Spring National Monument: Main Spring, Spring Room Spring, West Cabin Spring, and Tunnel Spring. Remains of Whitmore's dugout lie near Winsor Castle. National Park Service map, modified after Martin (2007).

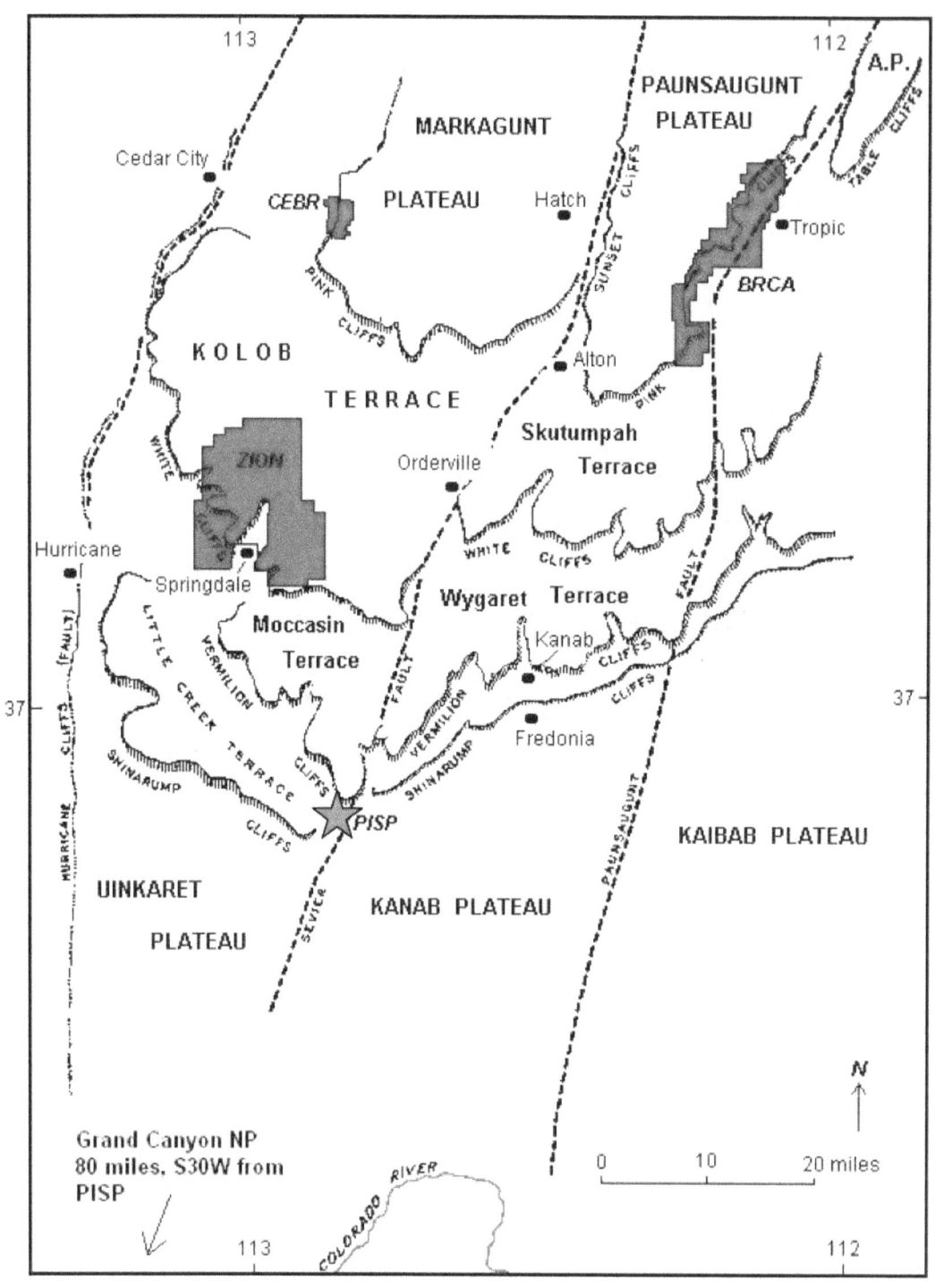

Figure 4. Regional location of Pipe Spring National Monument (PISP). Pipe Spring National Monument (red star) lies at the southern end of the Vermilion Cliffs, and the springs are located west of the Sevier Fault. All of the plateaus and faults shown on the map are part of the larger Colorado Plateau physiographic province. ZION: Zion National Park; CEBR: Cedar Breaks National Monument; BRCA: Bryce Canyon National Park. Modified from Gregory (1950).

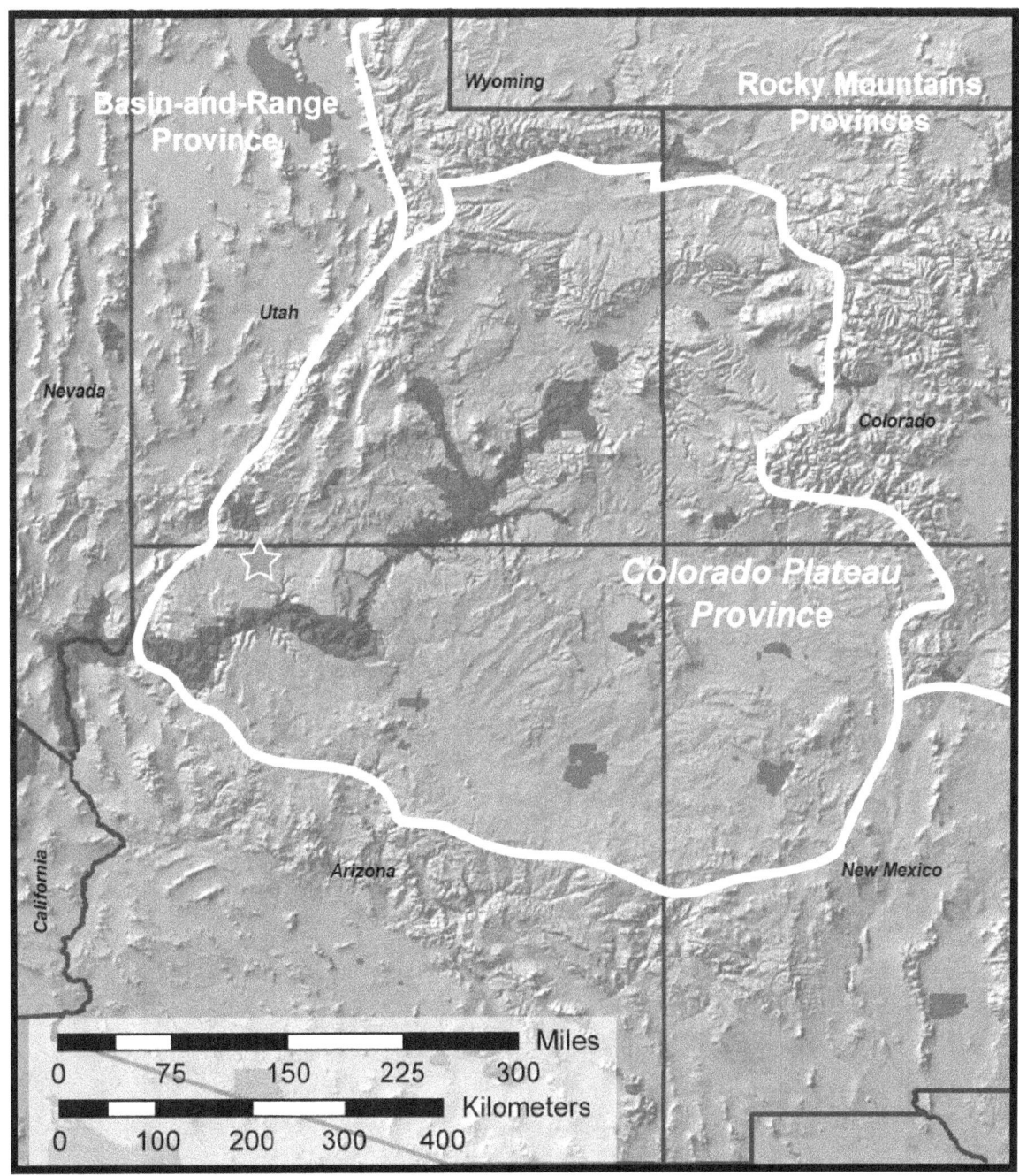

Figure 5. Shaded relief map showing National Park Service units (green) on the Colorado Plateau (outlined in white) and the immediate vicinity. Pipe Spring National Monument (red star) lies on the western margin of the Colorado Plateau. The Basin-and-Range Province, with its distinctive topography of narrow, north-south trending mountain ranges and basins, borders the Colorado Plateau to the northwest, west, and south. The Rocky Mountains Provinces border the Colorado Plateau to the northeast. Compiled from ESRI Arc Image Service, ESRI World Shaded Relief.

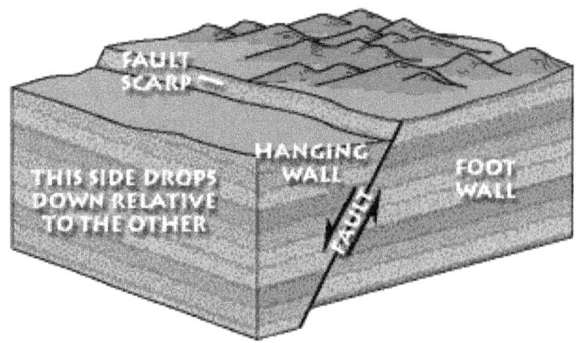

Normal Fault

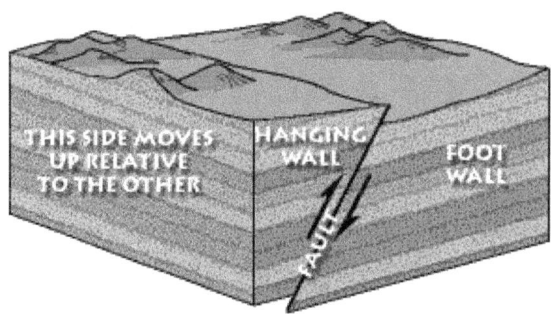

Reverse (thrust) Fault

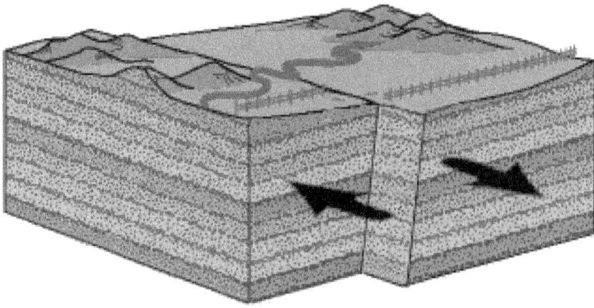

Strike-slip Fault

Figure 6. Diagrams of general fault types discussed in this report. In a "normal" fault (top diagram), rocks in the "hanging wall" above the fault plane move downward relative to rocks in the "footwall" below the fault plane. These terms developed as a result of early mining geology. Imagine walking down the fault plane in a mine. The rocks upon which you walk are in the "footwall" while those that hang above your head are in the "hanging wall." In a "reverse" fault (middle diagram), the hanging wall has moved up relative to the footwall. The only difference between a "reverse" fault and a "thrust" fault lies in the angle of the fault plane from the surface of the Earth. If the angle is more than about 15%, the fault is a "reverse" fault; if 15% or less, it's a "thrust" fault. In a reverse fault, compressive forces juxtapose older (underlying), hanging wall strata against younger, footwall strata. In "strike-slip" faulting, the rocks on each side of the fault slide laterally past each other. Strike-slip faulting usually contains elements of normal faulting and reverse faulting, as well. Diagrams are from the U.S. Geological Survey, http://geomaps.wr.usgs.gov/parks/deform/gfaults.html, accessed August 2009.

Figure 7. Monoclines on the Colorado Plateau. Typical of the large monoclines on the Colorado Plateau, the Island Monocline in Colorado National Monument has one gently dipping limb (Limb A) and one more steeply dipping limb (Limb B). The dip angle is the angle from a horizontal surface (line of white dots) to the yellow arrows, which approximate bedding surfaces in the sedimentary strata. Modified from a National Park Service/Sally Bellacqua photograph, http://www.nps.gov/colm/naturescience/ geologicformations.htm, accessed August, 2009.

Period	Formation/Map Unit (map symbol)	Thickness	General Description
Quaternary (Holocene)	Artificial fill (Qaf)	Variable	Alluvium and bedrock material used for construction projects other than highways
Quaternary (Holocene)	Surficial deposits (Qs, Qfp, Qps, Qes, Qae, Qv, Qtr, Qg1)	Variable	Unconsolidated alluvium; pebbles, sand, silt, and clay particles.
Quaternary (Holocene)	Eolian sand dune deposits (Qd)	Variable	Fine- to coarse-grained sand.
Quaternary (Holocene)	Young alluvial fan deposits (Qa1)	1.5 - 12 m (4.9-39 ft)	Light red, gray, and brown silt, fine- to coarse-grained inter-bedded sand and gravel; partly consolidated by gypsum, calcite, and clay.
Quaternary (Holocene and Pleistocene)	Intermediate alluvial deposits (Qg2, Qa2)	Variable	Terrace and alluvial fan deposits of interlayered clay, silt, and fine- to coarse-grained sand.
Quaternary (Holocene and Pleistocene)	Landslide debris deposits (Ql)	Variable	Detached blocks of strata.
Quaternary (Pleistocene)	Old alluvial deposits (Qg3, Qa3, QTg4)	Variable	Older terrace and alluvial fan deposits of interlayered clay, silt, sand, gravel, cobbles, and boulders.
	Regional Unconformity		
Jurassic (Lower)	Navajo Sandstone (Jn)*	457 m (1,500 ft)	White to light red and yellow-gray, cross-bedded, well-sorted, eolian (windblown) quartz sandstone inter-bedded with dark red sandstone and siltstone in the lower part.
Jurassic (Lower)	Tenney Canyon Tongue of the Kayenta Formation (Jkt)	37 – 67 m (120 - 220 ft)	Dark-red to light red-brown siltstone and sandstone.
Jurassic (Lower)	Lamb Point Tongue of the Navajo Sandstone (Jnl)*	43 - 120 m (140 - 400 ft)	Gray-white to orange-brown, cross-bedded quartz sandstone.
Jurassic (Lower)	Kayenta Formation (Jk)	82 - 122 m (270 - 400 ft)	Dark red and light red-brown, calcareous mudstone, siltstone, and sandstone.
Jurassic (Lower)	Moenave Formation (Jm, Jms, Jmw, Jmd)	90 - 137 m (295 - 449 ft)	Varicolored sandstone, siltstone and claystone.
	Regional Unconformity		
Triassic (Upper)	Chinle Formation (TRc, TRcp, TRcs)	186 - 248 m (610 - 814 ft)	Varicolored conglomerate, sandstone, siltstone, claystone, and limestone.
	Regional Unconformity		
Triassic (Lower)	Moenkopi Formation (TRm, TRmu, TRms, TRmm, TRmv, TRml)	186 - 217 m (610 - 712 ft)	Red-brown, thin-bedded gypsiferous siltstone and sandstone; white to light gray, laminated to thinly bedded, dolomite inter-bedded with light gray, calcareous silty gypsum; light-gray, thin-bedded to laminated limestone.
	Regional Unconformity		
Permian (Lower)	Kaibab Formation (Pk, Pkh, Pkf)	125 m (410 ft)	Red and gray siltstone, sandstone, and gypsum and gray limestone.

Figure 8. Stratigraphic column for Pipe Spring National Monument and vicinity. Units exposed in Pipe Spring National Monument are colored. The formations and members within the formations are explained in detail in the Map Unit Properties Table.

* = The interpretation of the Navajo Sandstone in the northwest corner of the monument by Billingsley and others (2004) as the main body of the Navajo Sandstone (Jn) is preferred over the description in Sharrow (2009) as the Lamb Point tongue (Jnl). (D. Sharrow, hydrologist, National Park Service, written communication, February 1, 2010).

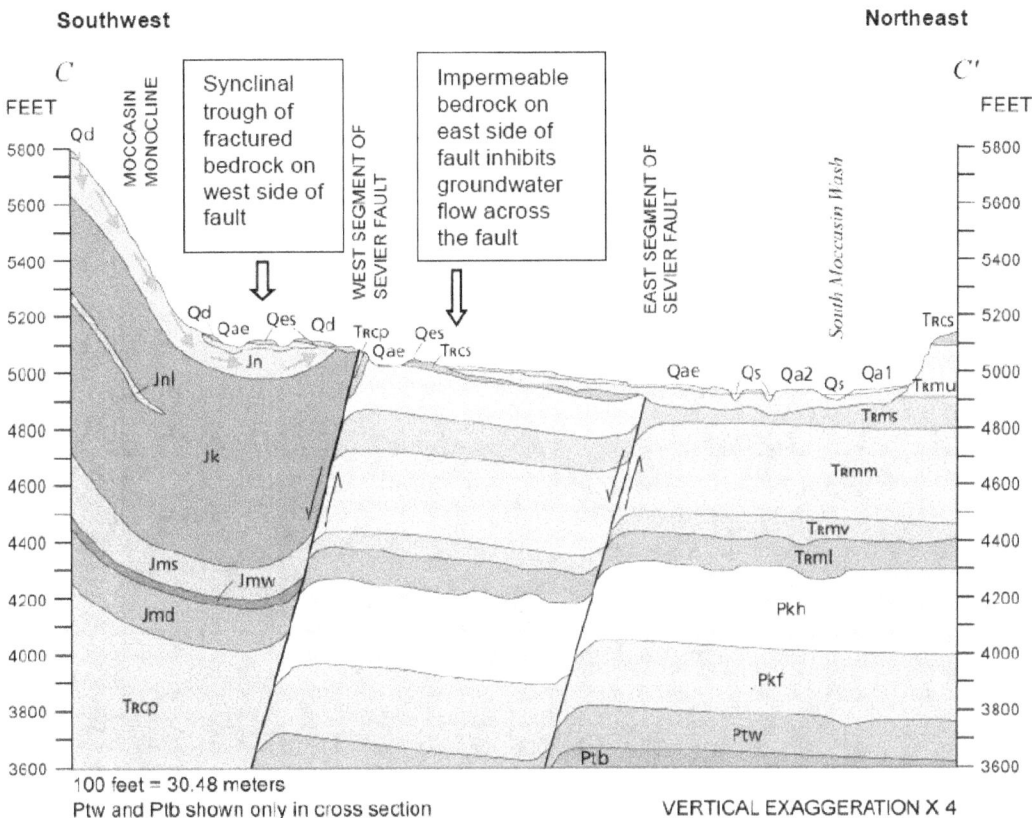

Figure 9. Southwest-to-northeast geologic cross section displaying an interpretation of the Moccasin Monocline, the associated syncline that formed west of the Sevier Fault, and the general subsurface geology in the Pipe Spring National Monument area. Groundwater (blue arrows) percolates through porous and fractured Navajo Sandstone (Jn) until it encounters the underlying, relatively impermeable Kayenta Formation (Jk). Groundwater flow is then directed downhill, into the syncline (the concave folded rock units) on the west side of the Sevier Fault. Impermeable strata east of the Sevier Fault inhibits groundwater flow across the fault, forcing groundwater to flow along bedding planes and fractures in the syncline until it intersects the land surface and emerges as springs, such as Pipe Spring and Moccasin Spring. The C – C' transect is located north of the monument, and the symbols for the rock strata are the same as those found on the map in Attachment 1. Quaternary (Q), Jurassic (J), Triassic (TR), and Permian (P) units significant to Pipe Spring National Monument are described in detail in the Map Unit Properties Table and throughout this report. Modified from Billingsley and others (2004), available at http://pubs.er.usgs.gov/usgspubs/sim/sim2863, accessed April 6, 2007.

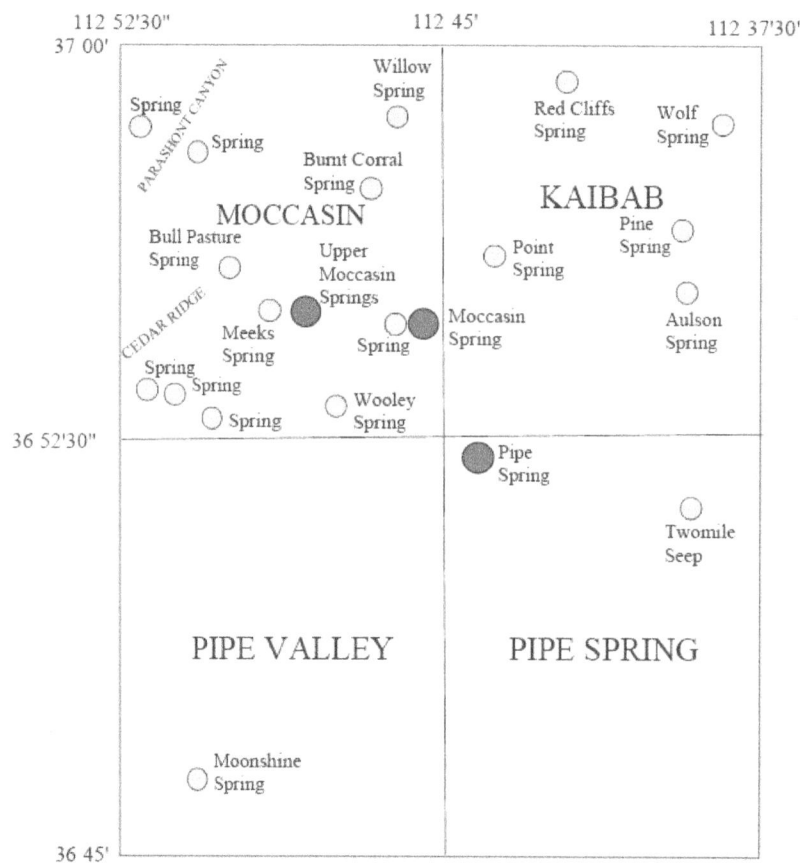

Figure 10. Location of springs shown on the Moccasin, Kaibab, Pipe Valley, and Pipe Spring U.S. Geological Survey 7.5-minute quadrangles, Mohave County, northern Arizona. Pipe Spring, Moccasin Spring, and Upper Moccasin Springs (marked in dark blue) generally have discharges greater than 4 lpm (>1 gpm). U.S. Geological Survey map modified from Billingsley and others (2004), available at http://pubs.er.usgs.gov/usgspubs/sim/sim2863, accessed April 6, 2007.

Figure 11. Petroglyphs carved into Navajo Sandstone. The dark coating on the surface of the sandstone is "desert varnish," a surface coating of manganese or iron oxide common to the deserts of the southwestern United States. National Park Service photograph.

Geologic Issues

The Geologic Resources Division held a Geologic Resources Inventory scoping session for Pipe Spring National Monument on June 28, 2001, to discuss geologic resources, address the status of geologic mapping, and assess resource management issues and needs. This section synthesizes the scoping results, in particular those issues that may require attention from resource managers.

The primary geologic issue facing park resource management is the sustainability of groundwater flow to the springs. Other issues include potential earthquake activity and the preservation of dinosaur footprints that were discovered in 1988. Additional information and references regarding physical resources and issues within Pipe Spring National Monument may be found in Sharrow (2009). Contact the Geologic Resources Division for technical assistance.

Spring Flow Sustainability

In the spring of 1971, the U.S. Geological Survey (USGS), under the direction of the National Park Service (NPS), drilled five test wells in an attempt to find a water supply to replace or supplement water from Pipe Spring. The wells were drilled in alluvium along Twomile and South Moccasin Washes, but they were either dry or produced poor-quality water. The NPS had little choice but to complete a water supply well in the Navajo Sandstone along the Sevier Fault, despite the possibility that pumping groundwater from the fault zone may cause flow from Pipe Spring to decline (McKoy 2000; Martin 2007).

Following completion of the NPS well in 1971, park staff noticed a decline in flow from the springs. In 1975, the Kaibab-Paiute Tribe determined that its original well at Kaibab Village was no longer adequate (McKoy 2000; Martin 2007). The Tribe completed a water supply well in 1980 at a location 200 m (700 ft) southwest of the NPS well. This well was also drilled along the Sevier Fault zone (fig. 12).

As a result of declining spring flow, the NPS initiated a routine spring flow monitoring program in July of 1976. Prior to this program, very few measurements from the springs had been collected (Martin 2007). The earliest NPS measurements occurred in September 1933 and May 1934, recording flows of 159 liters per minute (lpm) (42 gallons per minute; gpm) and 163 lpm (43 gpm), respectively. Four measurements between March 1959 and July 1976 recorded flows ranging from 121 lpm (32 gpm) to 144 lpm (38 gpm). Whether these reported flows represent the cumulative discharge from all of the spring outlets or only the flow from the springs at Winsor Castle is not known (Martin 2007).

Since July 1976, flows at West Cabin Spring, Tunnel Spring, and the cistern in the courtyard of the Castle have been measured at regular intervals. Flow at the cistern is the combined flow from Main Spring and Spring Room Spring. Monthly discharge data record a decreased

outflow from the springs from 1976 to 1985, primarily due to declining flow from the courtyard cistern. Flow from Tunnel Spring increased after 1990, but flow from the cistern decreased. Measurements were not collected at Tunnel Spring from September 1999 to September 2003, due to construction.

There has been no natural flow from Main Spring or Spring Room Spring since flow ceased from the courtyard cistern in 1999. Total spring flow at the monument averaged 49 lpm (13 gpm) from September 2003 to April 2007. Total spring flow primarily reflects flow from Tunnel Spring, as West Cabin Spring adds less than 2 lpm (0.5 gpm) to the total (Dave Sharrow, hydrologist, National Park Service, written communication, October 30, 2008). Monitoring data record a continuing trend of decreasing spring flow (Martin 2007).

Field mapping, computer modeling, and electromagnetic surveys have helped show that groundwater flow to the springs at Pipe Spring is controlled by the surrounding geologic structure (Billingsley et al. 2004; Truini et al. 2004; Sabol 2005; Martin 2007). The synclinal trough that parallels the West Branch of the Sevier Fault is a 300-490 m (1,000-1,600 ft) wide fracture zone of Navajo Sandstone that acts as a conduit for groundwater flow, directing flow from north to south. During reconstruction of Tunnel Spring in 2001, groundwater was seen seeping from fractures in the Kayenta Formation (fig. 13).

The groundwater flow system is impacted by geomorphology in addition to geologic structure. The east-west trending Moccasin Canyon intercepts the synclinal trough and divides the Navajo aquifer into two nearly separate systems north and south of the canyon (Martin 2007). The wash and the alluvium filling the wash cut across the saturated zone of the Navajo aquifer where the trough crosses Moccasin Wash (fig. 14). The alluvium that fills Moccasin Wash has a lower permeability than the fractured Navajo Sandstone so impedes groundwater flow from north to south. Some of the groundwater discharges at Moccasin Spring on the north side of Moccasin Wash, and some groundwater diverts to the east and exits the flow system associated with the Sevier Fault (Sabol 2005; Martin 2007). This groundwater is no longer available to the springs at Pipe Spring.

Moccasin Spring, which lies 5.6 km (3.5 mi) northwest of Pipe Spring (fig. 12), is a critical water source for

Moccasin, Arizona (Martin 2007). Assuming that both springs have the same groundwater source, the groundwater gradient between Moccasin Spring and Pipe Spring is about 11 m/km (57 ft/mi). Both springs discharge at the base of the east-dipping Moccasin Monocline, and are at or near the contact of the Navajo Sandstone and the Kayenta Formation (Billingsley et al. 2004). Like Pipe Spring, Moccasin Spring is associated with north-south and northwest-southeast oriented bedrock joints and fractures.

South of Moccasin Canyon, precipitation that infiltrates to the Navajo aquifer on Moccasin Mountain flows easterly and is concentrated in fractured rocks in the synclinal trough. Consequently, spring flow at Pipe Spring National Monument represents a small, local groundwater system limited to the little groundwater flow not captured by Moccasin Wash and to recharge from southern Moccasin Mountain, south of Moccasin Canyon (fig. 15) (Sabol 2005; Martin 2007).

Monitoring data from a number of studies have shown a clear correlation between groundwater pumping from the NPS and Tribal supply wells and the decline of flow from the springs (Martin 2007). Barrett and Williams (1986) concluded that the cumulative effects of groundwater pumping from wells along the Sevier Fault north of the monument caused spring flow to decline. Inglis (1990) found that water levels in the immediate vicinity of the NPS and Tribal supply wells declined about 2 m (5 ft) from 1971 to 1989. Continuous monitoring showed that water levels quickly recovered following a 24-hour pump test of the NPS and Tribal supply wells (Inglis 1997). Similar results were noted following a December 2006 pump test of the new NPS well, suggesting that the aquifer is relatively open and gives up water freely (Dave Sharrow, hydrologist, National Park Service, written communication, January 15, 2010). Barrett and Williams (1986) and Martin (2007) concluded that the decline in spring flow was related to pumping activity at the wells rather than natural variations in precipitation.

Water levels have been monitored since 1976 in a USGS monitoring well located north of the NPS and Tribal supply wells, and since 1989 in a NPS monitoring well drilled south of the supply wells (fig. 12). Water levels in these monitoring wells have declined about 0.1 m (0.3 ft) per year since the initiation of groundwater pumping. Seasonal fluctuations occur in both the NPS monitoring well (0.01 m; 0.04 feet) and spring discharge (7-11 lpm; 2-3 gpm) (Dave Sharrow, hydrologist, National Park Service, written communication, October 30, 2008).

If the NPS and Kaibab-Paiute Tribe continue to pump groundwater from their supply wells, discharge from the springs at the monument is likely to continue to decline, and eventually the springs will cease flowing (Martin 2007). Conversely, if pumping stops, spring flow should increase. Water levels in the aquifer would probably recover, and flow from the springs at Pipe Spring National Monument would probably increase, if the NPS and Tribal supply wells were relocated north of Moccasin, or if another source of water could be

imported into the area (Martin 2007). For additional details, refer to Sharrow (2009).

Groundwater Flow System: Research Opportunities

In 2002, seismic reflection and refraction surveys conducted north of the monument identified previously undetected faults. However, the faults were unlikely to contain much groundwater (Rymer et al. 2007; Martin 2007). A seismic -refraction survey in 2004 attempted to identify discrete fracture zones and local groundwater flow paths to individual spring openings (Truini et al. 2004). The data indicated that saturated conditions exist near West Cabin Spring and in an area east of Winsor Castle on Winsor Point. However, the survey was unable to resolve geologic features at the level of detail necessary to identify small fracture zones that partially control groundwater movement. Suggestions for future research included using direct resistivity methods to map the two-dimensional distribution of electrical properties within the monument. Such a map could better delineate faults and fractures, as well as relationships among these structures, groundwater movement and spring discharge (Truini et al. 2004).

During the summer and fall of 2007, two additional geophysical studies were conducted. In one study, a private contractor conducted an electrical resistivity survey in the Moccasin Mountain recharge area, about 10 km (6 mi) north of the monument (Mayerle and Urquhart 2008). A resistivity survey introduces an electric current into the ground and measures the difficulty with which the current flows through unconsolidated sediment and rock.

The object of the Moccasin Mountain survey was to map subsurface changes in resistivity as a way to identify changes in pore space and pore fluids. For example, resistivity of fractured, saturated bedrock often is lower than resistivity in unfractured surrounding material. Controlled Source Audio-frequency Magnetotellurics (CSAMT) geophysical data was acquired along two lines. Both lines showed similar results.

In general, the study identified a moderately resistant layer of Navajo Sandstone underlain by more resistant Jurassic sandstones, most probably the Kayenta Formation, that act as a barrier to downward percolation of groundwater. The high resistivity layer of Jurassic sandstone units rested above the more conductive Chinle Formation, buried to a depth of approximately 180-240 m (590-780 ft) below the surface on the eastern end of the survey lines. The data also indicate several possible water-filled fractures in the Kayenta Formation—a finding that is relevant to Pipe Spring National Monument. Further research using transient electromagnetic techniques (TEM) may be able to enhance the resolution of these fractures and detect the presence of water in the subsurface (Mayerle and Urquhart 2008).

A second study, conducted by the USGS, ran direct current resistivity transects in the vicinity of the springs to resolve the degree of fracturing and groundwater saturation in the immediate area. One transect crossed the tip of Winsor Point just upslope from the fort and the other two were east-west lines 0.8 km (0.5 mi) and 1.6 km (1 mi) north of the monument. The objective of the study is to delineate discrete fracture zones that may be pathways for groundwater flow to individual springs (Martin 2007; Dave Sharrow, hydrologist, National Park Service, written communication, October 4, 2007).

The amount of groundwater that flows from north to south across, or under, Moccasin Wash remains to be evaluated. Resolution of this issue would help identify the recharge area for the groundwater system feeding the spring. The question remains as to whether the cause of spring flow decline is almost entirely due to groundwater pumping from the NPS and Tribal supply wells, or if groundwater pumping at Moccasin and north of Moccasin significantly contributes to the decline of spring flow. An improved understanding of the geohydrology in this area would improve the ability to evaluate the benefits and risks of moving park and Tribal wells to a location north of Moccasin Wash.

Geochemical sampling of groundwater along with additional geophysical surveys may be useful in determining the degree of separation or interconnection of groundwater in the fracture zone north and south of Moccasin Wash. Again, this information would help determine if relocating wells to the area north of Moccasin would impact groundwater levels south of Moccasin Wash.

Potential Seismic (Earthquake) Hazards

Ground shaking caused by movement on the north-south trending Sevier Fault that bisects Pipe Spring National Monument may disrupt the groundwater flow system by closing or opening fractures. Faulting may also realign the lateral juxtaposition of impermeable beds against permeable Navajo Sandstone. In addition, the west corner of Winsor Castle is built on the west (downward moving) side of the Sevier Fault while the east corner is on the fault's east (upward moving) side.

Most of the 400 m (1,300 ft) of normal fault displacement along the Sevier Fault occurred between 5.3 million years and 10,000 years ago, during Pliocene and Pleistocene time (Billingsley et al. 2004). At Black Mountain, approximately 50 km (30 mi) north of Pipe Spring, estimates of vertical slip rates on the Sevier Fault from the middle Miocene (15 million years ago) to the present range from 0.03 mm/year (0.001 in/year) to 0.07 mm/year (0.003 in/year) (Lund et al. 2008). South of Pipe Spring National Monument, middle Quaternary (1 million years ago) displacement rates for the Sevier/Toroweap Fault where it crosses the western Grand Canyon range from 0.07 mm/year (0.003 in/year) to 0.18 mm/year (0.007 in/year) (Fenton et al. 2001). The current vertical slip rate along the Sevier Fault in Utah is <0.1 mm/year (Lund et al. 2008).

To put these slippage rates into perspective, displacement rates on the Sevier Fault are similar to those for the Hurricane Fault, where the seismic hazard is more recognized. They are one-hundredth the slip rate of the San Andreas Fault.

The Sevier Fault has the capability of producing a magnitude 7.3 - 7.5 earthquake. However, large earthquakes with magnitudes of 6.5 - 7.5 on the Richter scale are rare in this area. The 1992 St. George earthquake recorded a magnitude of 5.8. Since 1987, more than 40 earthquakes with magnitudes greater or equal to 2.5 have occurred in northwestern Arizona, including the magnitude 5.4 Cataract Canyon earthquake, which occurred between Flagstaff, Arizona, and the Grand Canyon in 1993 (Lund et al. 2002). These earthquakes did not rupture the surface at Pipe Spring National Monument.

Estimating the recurrence interval of major earthquakes capable of breaking the surface involves considerable uncertainty because of the low slip rates. Because the slip rates are so low, many years are required to build up sufficient stress to produce a major surface-rupturing earthquake. The average recurrence interval for surface faulting on the active Hurricane Fault (northwest Arizona and southwest Utah) ranges from several thousand to possibly more than 10,000 years. Slippage along the Sevier Fault at Black Mountain occurred every 4,400 to 5,300 years during the late Pleistocene, but the current recurrence interval between surface-faulting earthquakes on the Sevier Fault is estimated to be at least ~30,000 years (Lund et al. 2008).

Furthermore, the lengthy Sevier/Toroweap Fault appears to be broken into seismic segments that may move independently of one another (Lund et al. 2008). Recent movement on the Sevier Fault segment near Pipe Spring National Monument has been less than movements on segments to the north, near Panguich, Utah, or segments to the south at Grand Canyon (Dave Sharrow, hydrologist, National Park Service, written communication, October 30, 2008).

The age of the last large earthquake to disrupt Pipe Spring National Monument is unknown. The lack of a surface scarp in the vicinity suggests that a large earthquake has not occurred in an exceptionally long time. All of Pipe Spring National Monument is within the potential zone of deformation that would occur from a large earthquake. Surface rupture along the fault could be very destructive.

Preservation of Dinosaur Footprints

In 1988, three dinosaur footprints were discovered 2 m (6 ft) above the base of the Navajo Sandstone within Pipe Spring National Monument (fig. 16) (Stokes 1988; Cuffey et al. 1998; Santucci et al. 1998). The tracks are imprints from a tridactyl (three-toed) therapod, a bipedal carnivore with grasping hands and clawed digits. Suggestions in 1998 to manage and interpret the footprints included the following (Cuffey et al. 1998):

- Add an exhibit in the Visitor Center and a plaque at the site of the footprints,

- Install a protective fence or railing around the tracks,

- Produce a site bulletin

Since 1998, all wayside exhibits at Pipe Spring National Monument have been updated, so the stratigraphic error that labeled the Kayenta Formation as Chinle has been corrected. No other action has occurred regarding the

tracks (Dave Sharrow, hydrologist, National Park Service, written communication, October 4, 2007). Monitoring strategies for in situ paleontological resources are suggested by Santucci and others (2009).

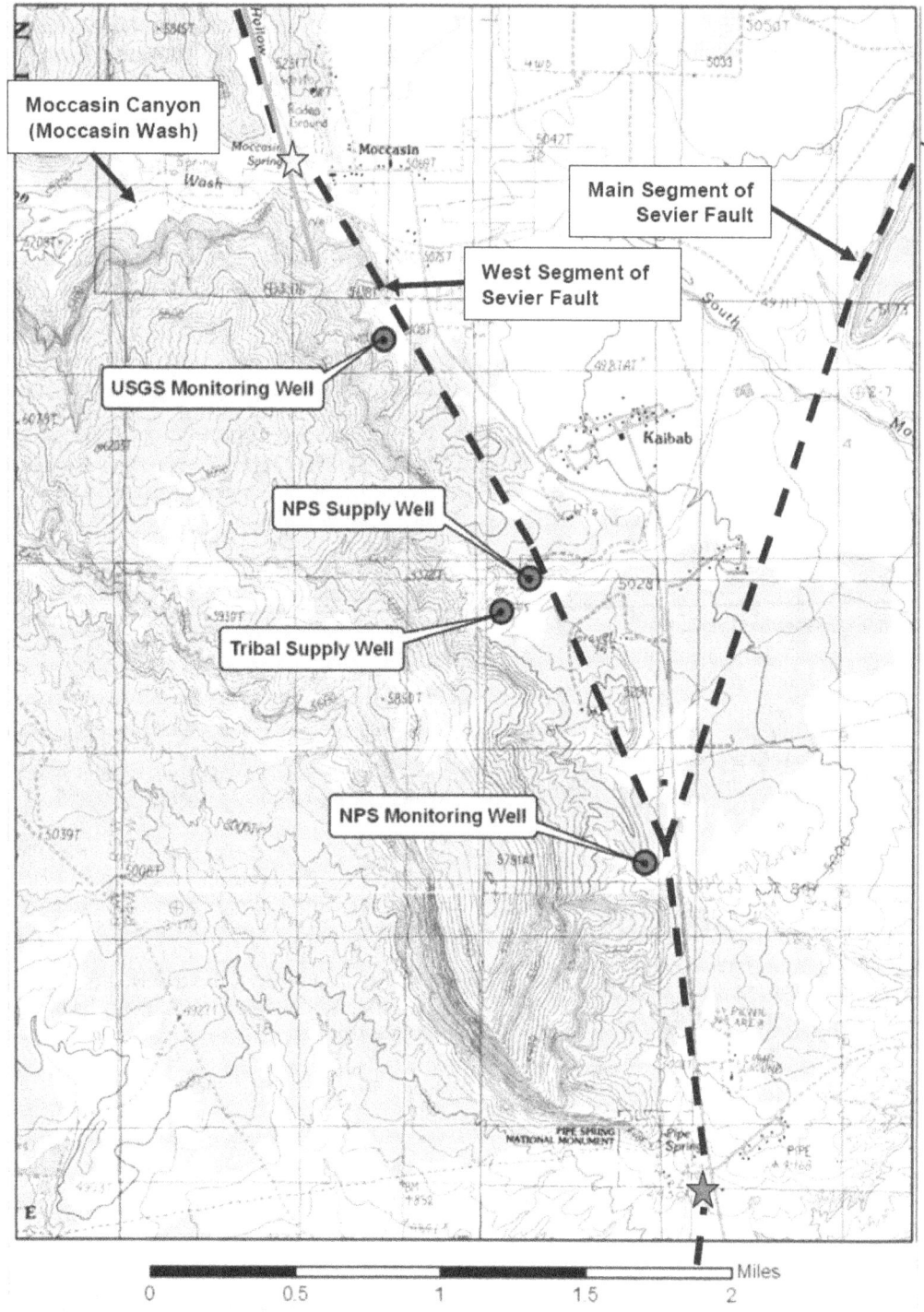

Figure 12. Location of water level monitoring wells and water supply wells near Pipe Spring (red star). Water levels have been measured at the USGS monitoring well since 1976, and at the NPS monitoring well since 1989. Moccasin Canyon intercepts the syncline that parallels the west segment of the Sevier Fault (dashed line) and some groundwater is diverted to Moccasin Spring (yellow star). The blue line that cuts Moccasin Spring marks the location of the cross-section presented in figure 14. National Park Service graphic modified from Martin (2007).

Figure 13. Fractured bedrock provides a conduit for groundwater flow to Pipe Spring. Vertical fractures and joints cut the Jurassic sandstone that crops out on Winsor Point in the upper photograph. Buried in the syncline west of the Sevier Fault (fig. 9), these fractures provide a conduit for groundwater flow. In the lower photograph, groundwater seeps from fractured bedrock in the upper layers of the Kayenta Formation in the open adit, or horizontal passageway, during reconstruction of Tunnel Spring in 2001. Upper photograph by Dave Sharrow, hydrologist, National Park Service. Lower photograph modified from Truini and others (2004; courtesy Margot Truini, U.S. Geological Survey)

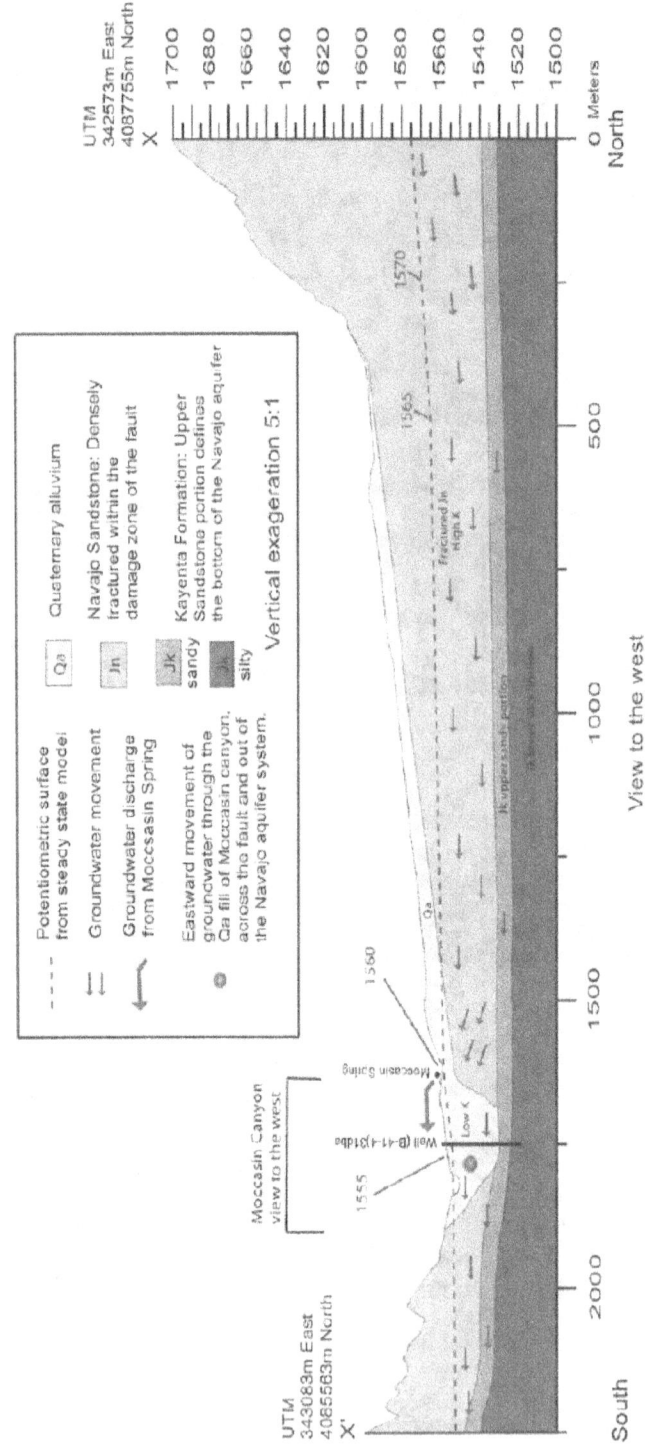

Figure 14. South to north cross-section showing groundwater flow (blue arrows) from north to south in the fractured rock associated with the west segment of the Sevier Fault. Groundwater flows through fractured Navajo Sandstone (Jn) until it reaches a low permeability (k) zone in Moccasin Canyon alluvium, which impedes groundwater flow. Some of the groundwater emerges at Moccasin Spring; some is intercepted by the sediments filling Moccasin Wash and flows into valley alluvium to the east; and some of the groundwater continued to flow south toward the NPS and Tribal potable supply wells and eventually Pipe Spring. The location of cross-section X-X' is indicated by the blue line in figure 12. Modified from Sabol (2005).

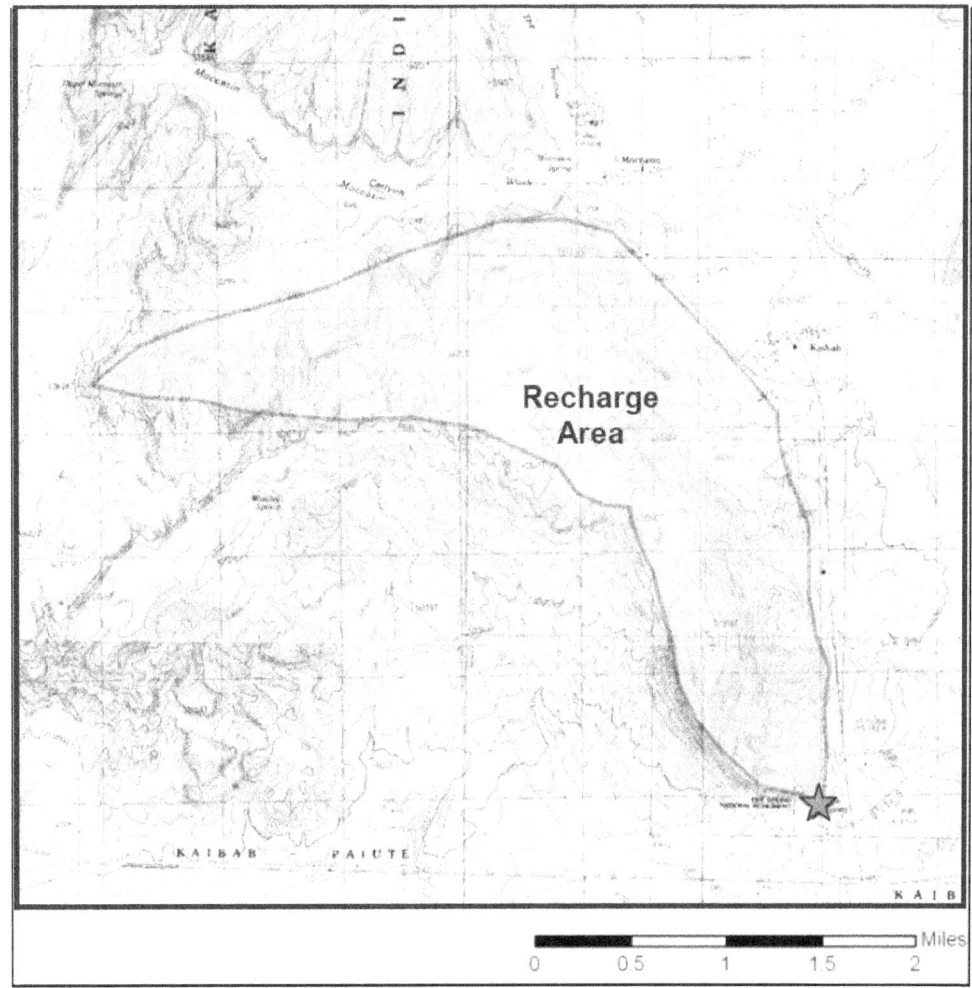

Figure 15. Possible recharge area (shaded green) for the springs at Pipe Spring National Monument (red star). Modified from Martin (2007) and Sabol (2005).

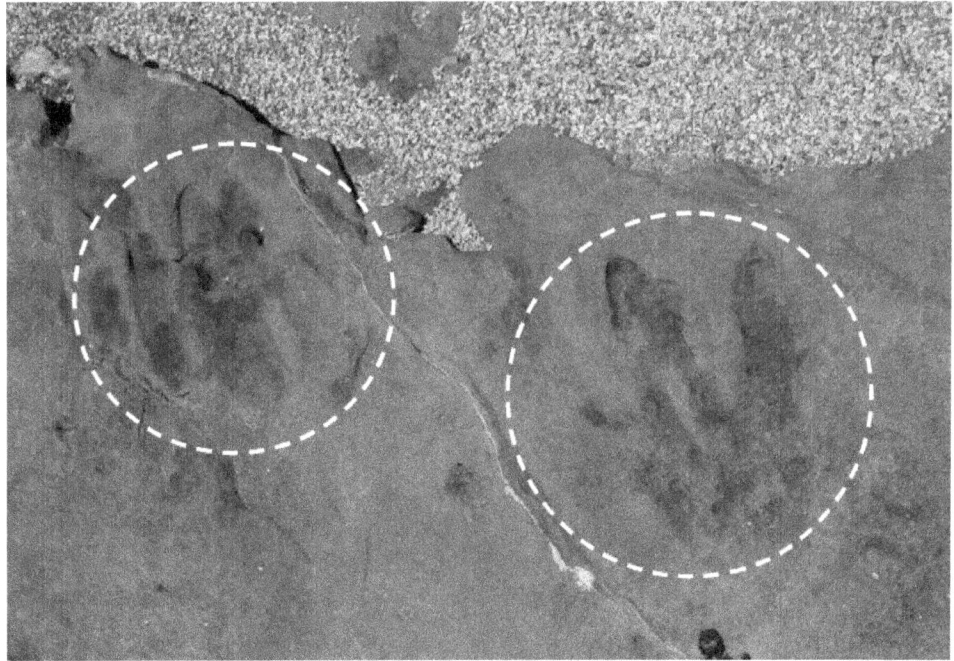

Figure 16. Dinosaur footprints (circled) in the Navajo Sandstone within Pipe Spring National Monument. The right footprint is about 30 cm (12 in) long toe tip to heel. National Park Service photograph courtesy Andrea Bornemeier (Pipe Spring NM).

Figure 17. Winsor Castle in 1907, following the construction of Main Spring and Spring Room Spring. National Park Service photograph courtesy Andrea Bornemeier (Pipe Spring NM).

Figure 18. View of restored Winsor Castle and pond. Spring water was discharged from Winsor Castle into the pond. Much of the building stone for the historic structures was obtained from the red rocks of the Kayenta Formation. National Park Service photograph courtesy Andrea Bornemeier (Pipe Spring NM).

Geologic Features and Processes

This section describes the most prominent and distinctive geologic features and processes in Pipe Spring National Monument.

Springs

The four springs within Pipe Spring National Monument (fig. 3) sustained early human settlement in the area and provided the catalyst for national monument status. Main Spring and Spring Room Spring are not natural springs; they were constructed between 1870 and 1900 by Mormon pioneers (figs. 17 and 18). As historically configured, a cistern in the courtyard of Winsor Castle gathered water from Spring Room Spring, located under the Parlor in the western corner of the structure. From the cistern, water was piped into the Spring Room, providing cooling for cheese-making that occurred there. The water was then discharged out of the building and into the ponds. A subsurface bark-lined channel connected the cistern with Main Spring, which is a short distance south of the fort walls. The Main Spring pool also may have received direct groundwater inflow.

Drilled into the hillside between 1902 and 1907, Tunnel Spring is a horizontal passage that captures groundwater as it moves slowly through the aquifer (fig. 13). West Cabin Spring (previously known as Calf Pasture Spring) is a small, undeveloped spring located on the hillside above West Cabin (Truini et al. 2004; Martin 2007).

The configuration of spring flow in the historic Winsor Castle structure changed in 2002 after discharge from Main Spring and Spring Room Spring ceased. The tunnel of Tunnel Spring was stabilized in 2000 to protect what had become the primary spring. Since the stabilization, water has been pumped from Tunnel Spring up to the Spring Room and ponds.

Springs may occur where faults block the lateral movement of groundwater, or where permeable rock has been removed by erosion. At Pipe Spring National Monument, both conditions occur. The porous Navajo Sandstone and the upper sandstone layers of the Kayenta Formation have been folded, fractured, and offset by the north-south trending Sevier Fault. The high-angle, west-dipping fault plane of the Sevier Fault acts as a partial barrier to the eastward flow of groundwater. Abundant claystone and gypsum in the Chinle and Moenkopi Formations east of the Sevier Fault are relatively impermeable and prevent groundwater leakage through the fault. Groundwater accumulates on the west side of the fault and is forced to flow along the bedding planes and fractures in the sandstone until it intersects the land surface and emerges as spring flow. Thus, spring discharge at Pipe Spring represents the overflow at the lower extremity of a groundwater system, at the point where the fractured permeable rocks that carry the water intersect the surface topography (fig. 9).

Sevier Fault

The Sevier Fault originally formed in the Mesozoic Era as a reverse fault. While normal faults form from extension of the crust, reverse faults are generated by compression of the crust (fig. 6). Strata above the fault plane in a reverse fault have moved up and over strata below the fault plane. During the Jurassic-to-Cretaceous Sevier Orogeny (mountain-building episode), easterly-directed compressive forces emplaced Paleozoic strata from California and western Nevada onto younger Mesozoic strata in Arizona, Utah, and eastern Nevada. The Sevier Fault is the ramp-like contact between the base of these older rocks and the younger strata.

In the Late Miocene, about 15 million years ago, the crust in the southwestern United States began to be pulled apart. Crustal stretching generated the regional, north-south trending normal faults that border the mountain ranges and adjacent basins of today's Basin-and-Range province. When the crust began to be pulled apart, the Sevier Fault was reactivated as a normal fault.

Evidence of the Sevier Fault is present in the vicinity of Pipe Spring, although the fault trace is not directly visible in the monument (fig. 19). The Shinarump Member of the Chinle Formation is displaced about 73 m (240 ft) along the main segment of the Sevier Fault, near South Moccasin Wash, 3 km (2 mi) north of the junction of the main segment and the west segment. The resulting escarpment forms a colorful slope of red Moenkopi Formation, capped by white sandstone of the Shinarump Member of the Chinle Formation. A segment of the Sevier Fault is partly visible between landslide deposits at the base of the Vermilion Cliffs, about 5 km (3 mi) north of South Moccasin Wash. Farther to the north, poor exposures of the fault are present in small drainages southwest of Blue Knolls, where the fault surface appears to dip west about 70° to 75° (Billingsley et al. 2004). The main segment of the Sevier Fault parallels the east-facing Vermilion Cliffs to Sandy Canyon Wash, where it then continues north into Utah, east of Coral Pink Sand Dunes State Park.

South of the monument, fluvial and eolian deposits obscure the fault because erosion of soft, easily-eroded rocks on both sides of the fault has worn the land surface evenly, although several hundred feet of displacement has occurred across the fault. Strata exposed on the east side of the fault in a drainage 1.6 km (1 mi) south of the monument dip west, into the fault, by as much as 45°. The Sevier Fault bends to the southwest and connects to the north-south trending Toroweap Fault about 40 km (25 mi) south of Pipe Spring (Billingsley et al. 2004).

Moccasin Monocline and Syncline

Monoclines on the Colorado Plateau (fig. 7), such as Moccasin Monocline, developed in response to the Late Cretaceous to mid-Eocene Laramide Orogeny. The Laramide Orogeny was another mountain-building episode resulting from the collision of the North American continent with the oceanic plate to the west. In contrast to the older Sevier Orogeny, the Laramide Orogeny displaced not only Paleozoic strata, but also deep crustal blocks of Precambrian rock. Reverse or thrust fault displacement occurred primarily along pre-existing Precambrian fault zones (Huntoon 2003; Billingsley et al. 2004). Strata above these deep-rooted thrust planes were folded into graceful monoclinal landforms like Moccasin Monocline.

The syncline that acts as a conduit for groundwater flow lies at the base of Moccasin Monocline (fig. 19). A flexure in the Vermilion Cliffs, just west of Pipe Spring, is the subtle topographic expression of this syncline (Billingsley et al. 2004). The Sevier Fault, Moccasin Monocline, and associated syncline all trend parallel to the west side of the paved road between Pipe Spring National Monument and Moccasin, Arizona. About 3 km (2 mi) north of Pipe Spring, the monocline and syncline gradually die out into Moccasin Mountain. The monocline and syncline also gradually disappear southwest of Pipe Spring.

Stratigraphic Features

The multicolored bands of Triassic and Jurassic strata that are visible from the monument contain a variety of sedimentary features. Ancient ripple marks and mudcracks have been preserved in the reddish-brown and greenish-gray, Lower Triassic Moenkopi Formation. White layers of gypsum are found among the dolomite, claystone, and siltstone of the Shnabkaib Member.

Cross-bedded sandstones characterize the Shinarump Member of the overlying, Upper Triassic Chinle Formation, which is exposed east of Pipe Spring in the Shinarump Cliffs. The Petrified Forest Member of the Chinle Formation contains petrified wood in the Blue Knolls area (Billingsley et al. 2004). Conglomerate and sandstone fill river channels that eroded into underlying sediment during the Triassic.

Cross-beds, fossilized plant remains, fish scales, algal laminations, and rip-up clasts (semi-consolidated mud eroded by a high-energy flow) are present in the Jurassic Moenave Formation. The thick-bedded sandstone of the Springdale Sandstone Member forms the conspicuous layer along the bottom one-third of the Vermilion Cliffs.

The dark red and light red-brown calcareous mudstone, siltstone, and sandstone of the Kayenta Formation record river channels, floodplains, and shallow lake environments that characterized the region prior to inundation by Navajo sand dunes. High-angle, cross-bedded sandstone is the prominent sedimentary feature in the cliff-forming Navajo Sandstone. These cross-beds represent ancient sand dunes that were once part of an extensive sand sea, or erg, that spread across Utah and

Arizona. In Zion National Park, north of the monument, exposures of the main body of Navajo Sandstone display this world-renowned cross-bedding. At Pipe Spring National Monument, the Navajo Sandstone forms an erosion-resistant cap above the Kayenta Formation (fig. 20).

Paleontology

The three tridactyl dinosaur footprints preserved within Pipe Spring National Monument lie in an orange-red, cross-bedded sandstone 2 m (6 ft) above the base of the Early Jurassic Navajo Sandstone (fig. 16) (Santucci et al. 1998; Cuffey et al. 1998). Preservation is poor, but the footprints have been identified as belonging to the fossil footprint genus *Eubrontes*, a name which means "true thunder." The fossil footprint species has not yet been determined, but reasonable possibilities include *Eubrontes approximatus, Eubrontes divaricatus, Eubrontes giganteus, Eubrontes platypus,* or *Eubrontes tuberatus* (Cuffey et al. 1998).

The actual dinosaur that created the *Eubrontes* footprints is currently unknown. No skeletal remains have ever been found associated with *Eubrontes* tracks, either at Pipe Spring or any other site where *Eubrontes* prints have been discovered (Coffey et al. 1998). The size of the tracks at Pipe Spring suggests that they are the prints of a moderately large theropod. The best-preserved print at Pipe Spring National Monument (fig. 16) measures 30 cm (12 in) long from toe-tip to heel and about as wide between the tips of the two lateral toes.

Eubrontes footprints are best known from the Connecticut River Valley in Massachusetts, where they were discovered in 1802. Once thought to be restricted to eastern North America, *Eubrontes* tracks have been frequently identified in sandstones on the Colorado Plateau (Lockley and Hunt 1994).

Structural Graben (Basin)

An unusual graben, or structural basin bounded by normal faults, has formed in the Vermilion Cliffs 3 km (2 mi) north of Kaibab, Arizona (Billingsley et al. 2004). The north-south trending graben cuts through the southeast tip of Moccasin Mountain, where the Navajo Sandstone records about 60 m (200 ft) of normal-fault offset. At its northern end, the graben turns sharply east toward the Sevier Fault. Displacement at its northern extension is about 49 m (160 ft).

Faulted down into the graben, the Navajo Sandstone slid southward on a surface of mudstone and siltstone in the lower part of the Kayenta Formation. As they slid, the sandstone beds in the landslide rotated backward so that when they came to rest, they dipped to the north towards the wall from which they detached. The normal faults terminate within the mudstones and siltstones of the Kayenta Formation.

Joints and Fractures

Joints and fractures break the limestone units of the Kaibab Formation and the hard sandstones found in the Navajo Sandstone, Kayenta Formation, Shinarump

Member of the Chinle Formation, and Springdale Sandstone Member of the Moenave Formation (fig. 20). In Moccasin Canyon and Moccasin Mountain, northwest of Pipe Spring National Monument, joints and fractures have four orientations: north-south, northeast, northwest, and east-west. The two most common joint sets are oriented northeast and northwest (Billingsley et al. 2004).

Open cracks in the canyon walls in Moccasin Canyon formed from the abundant northwest- and north-oriented joints and fractures in the Navajo Sandstone. The joint and fracture planes parallel the trend of the Moccasin Monocline.

Collapse Structures

Circular bowl-shaped features with inward-dipping strata have been mapped in the Pipe Spring area and identified as collapse structures. Dissolution of the

deeply buried Mississippian (359-318 million years ago) Redwall Limestone or dissolution of gypsum from the shallower Permian (299-251 million years ago) Kaibab or Toroweap Formations caused overlying strata to collapse inward. Some of the collapse structures resulting from dissolution of Redwall Limestone contain potential economic high-grade ore deposits of copper and uranium minerals (Billingsley et al. 2004).

One large collapse structure has been mapped in the upper reaches of Cove Canyon, northeast of Pipe Spring National Monument and about 5 km (3 mi) east of Kaibab, Arizona. This potentially deep feature is about 200 m (660 ft) in diameter. No collapse structures that might be identified on NPS or Tribal lands would be available for mineral exploration (Dave Sharrow, hydrologist, National Park Service, written communication, October 30, 2008).

Figure 19. Photograph showing the main segment of the Sevier Fault (black), the west branch of the fault (yellow, dashed where the fault trace trends behind the outcrop of Jurassic sandstone beds), and the syncline that parallels the west branch of the Sevier Fault (orange). Thin black arrows indicate the dip direction of the sandstone beds towards the center of the syncline. View is to the north. Pipe Spring National Monument lies south of the photograph. Photograph courtesy of Dave Sharrow, hydrologist, National Park Service.

Figure 20. Geologic contact (white line) between the Navajo Sandstone (Jn) and the Kayenta Formation (Jk), fractures (white arrows) in the Kayenta Formation, and a bedding plane (yellow arrows) in the Kayenta Formation, Pipe Spring National Monument, northern Arizona. Blocks of Navajo and Kayenta sandstone that have broken along fractures lie at the base of the cliff. U.S. Geological Survey photograph courtesy of Margot Truini.

Map Unit Properties

This section identifies characteristics of map units that appear on the Geologic Resources Inventory digital geologic map of Pipe Spring National Monument. The accompanying table is highly generalized and for background purposes only. Ground-disturbing activities should not be permitted or denied on the basis of information in this table.

Geologic maps facilitate an understanding of Earth, its processes, and the geologic history responsible for its formation. Hence, the geologic map for Pipe Spring National Monument informed the "Geologic History," "Geologic Features and Processes," and "Geologic Issues" sections of this report. Geologic maps are essentially two-dimensional representations of complex three-dimensional relationships. The various colors on geologic maps illustrate the distribution of rocks and unconsolidated deposits. Bold lines that cross or separate the color patterns mark structures such as faults and folds. Point symbols indicate features such as dipping strata, sample localities, mines, wells, and cave openings.

Incorporation of geologic data into a Geographic Information System (GIS) increases the usefulness of geologic maps by revealing the spatial relationships to other natural resources and anthropogenic features. Geologic maps are indicators of water resources because they show which rock units are potential aquifers and are useful for finding seeps and springs. Geologic maps do not show soil types and are not soil maps, but they do show parent material, a key factor in soil formation. Furthermore, resource managers have used geologic maps to make connections between geology and biology; for instance, geologic maps have served as tools for locating sensitive, threatened, and endangered plant species, which may prefer a particular rock unit.

Although geologic maps do not show where earthquakes will occur, the presence of a fault indicates past movement and possible future seismic activity. Geologic maps do not show where the next landslide, rockfall, or volcanic eruption will occur, but mapped deposits show areas that have been susceptible to such geologic hazards. Geologic maps do not show archaeological or cultural resources, but past peoples may have inhabited or been influenced by various geomorphic features that are shown on geologic maps. For example, alluvial terraces may preserve artifacts, and formerly inhabited alcoves may occur at the contact between two rock units.

The geologic units listed in the following table correspond to the accompanying digital geologic data. Map units are listed in the table from youngest to oldest. Please refer to the geologic time scale (fig. 21) for the age associated with each time period. This table highlights characteristics of map units such as susceptibility to hazards; the occurrence of fossils, cultural resources, mineral resources, and caves; and the suitability as habitat or for recreational use.

The GRI digital geologic maps reproduce essential elements of the source maps including the unit descriptions, legend, map notes, graphics, and report. The following reference is source data for the GRI digital geologic map for Pipe Spring National Monument:

Billingsley, G.H., S.S. Priest, and T.J. Felger. 2004. *Geologic map of Pipe Spring National Monument and the western Kaibab-Paiute Indian Reservation, Mohave County, Arizona*. Scale 1:31,680. Geologic Investigations Series Map I-2863. Reston, VA: U.S. Geological Survey.

The GRI team implements a geology-GIS data model that standardizes map deliverables. This data model dictates GIS data structure including data layer architecture, feature attribution, and data relationships within ESRI ArcGIS software, increasing the overall quality and utility of the data. GRI digital geologic map products include data in ESRI shapefile and coverage GIS formats, Federal Geographic Data Committee (FGDC)-compliant metadata, a help file that contains all of the ancillary map information and graphics, and an ESRI ArcMap map document file that easily displays the map with appropriate symbology. GRI digital geologic data are included on the attached CD and are available through the NPS Data Store (http://science.nature.nps.gov/nrdata/).

Geologic History

This section describes the rocks and unconsolidated deposits that appear on the digital geologic map of Pipe Spring National Monument, the environment in which those units were deposited, and the timing of geologic events that created the present landscape.

This section summarizes the tectonic and depositional history recorded in the strata within and surrounding Pipe Spring National Monument. The tectonic history includes two major orogenic (mountain-building) events: one that occurred in the Mesozoic, and one that began in the Mesozoic and ended in the Tertiary. Although the rocks in the Pipe Spring area record only a brief portion of Earth's geologic past, from the Permian Period (approximately 299 million years ago) to the present (fig. 21), they represent a wide variety of depositional environments and dynamic processes that shaped today's landscape.

Permian Period (299–251 million years ago)

About 270 million years ago, Pipe Spring National Monument lay just north of the Permian equator on the western margin of Pangaea, the supercontinent that formed as the globe's landmasses sutured together (fig. 22) (Biek et al. 2000; Morris et al. 2000). A dry, high atmospheric pressure climatic belt prevailed in this western part of Pangaea and resulted in restricted marine conditions over much of the cratonic shelf seaway (Peterson 1980). Warm, shallow seas and sabkhas (broad, very flat surfaces near sea level) covered the area. Farther to the west, a complex island arc assemblage formed above a subduction zone as lithospheric plates collided and dense oceanic crust descended beneath the less dense continental shelf and slope (Silberling and Roberts 1962). To the east, highlands in Colorado remain as remnants of the Ancestral Rocky Mountains that originated with the suturing of South America to North America in the Pennsylvanian.

During the Early Permian, the sea advanced (transgressed) and retreated (regressed) across northern Arizona and southwestern Utah, leaving open marine, restricted marine, sabkha, and eolian (wind) sediments that became the Toroweap Formation (Rawson et al. 1980). Gypsum in the Woods Ranch Member and Seligman Member reflects hot, dry conditions promoting evaporation at the time of deposition, while the fossiliferous limestone in the Brady Canyon Member records a transgression of the sea into the region. In Grand Canyon National Park, the Toroweap limestones contain fossils of brachiopods, crinoids, corals, and bryozoans. These invertebrates lived in well-oxygenated marine environments. However, the fetid odor present on fresh surfaces of Brady Canyon Member limestones in Kanab Canyon, south of the monument, suggests that a restricted, oxygen-depleted marine environment existed in this area at one time. The fetid odor results from accumulated organic material. In an oxygen-rich environment, benthic organisms typically assimilate any organic matter that settles through the water column.

The Kaibab Limestone records the last in a long series of Paleozoic seas that transgressed over the region. Fossiliferous, sandy limestone and gypsum indicate deposition under shallow, near-shore, warm and arid climatic conditions. The sea moved back and forth across northern Arizona and western Utah, but by the Middle Permian, the sea had withdrawn and the Kaibab Limestone was subaerially exposed to erosion. Dissolution of the Kaibab created karst topography, a landscape dotted with sinkholes, caves, and dissolution tunnels (Morris et al. 2000).

The close of the Permian brought the third, and most severe, major mass extinction of geologic time. Although not as famous as the extinction event at the end of the Mesozoic, the Permian extinction was much more extensive. An estimated 96% of all species were eliminated at the end of the Permian (Raup 1991). According to one hypothesis, a comet, about 6-13 km (4-8 mi) in diameter, collided with Earth (Becker et al. 2001). Such an impact may have triggered vast volcanic eruptions that spread lava over an area two-thirds the size of the United States.

Powerful updrafts would have carried dust and grit swirling into the upper atmosphere. The particulate matter would have reflected and scattered sunlight, resulting in years of global cooling, with freezing temperatures even during summertime. The sulfuric emissions from the volcanism would have mixed with atmospheric water to produce downpours of corrosive acid rain. Thousands of species of insects, reptiles, and amphibians died out on land, while in the oceans, coral formations vanished, as did snails, urchins, sea lilies, some fish, and the once-prolific trilobites.

Triassic Period (251–199.6 million years ago)

During the Triassic, Pangaea reached its greatest size. All the continents had come together to form a single landmass that was located symmetrically about the equator (Dubiel 1994). To the west, explosive volcanoes arose from the sea and formed a north-south trending arc of islands along the border of what is now California and Nevada (fig. 23) (Christiansen et al. 1994; Dubiel 1994; Lawton 1994).

The Lower Triassic Moenkopi Formation is a mix of fluvial, mudflat, sabkha, and shallow marine environments that developed from eastern Utah to eastern Nevada (fig. 23) (Stewart et al. 1972a; Christiansen et al. 1994; Doelling 2000; Huntoon et al. 2000). The basal member of the Moenkopi fills broad, east-flowing channels that incised into the Kaibab Limestone prior to the Triassic (Biek et al. 2000). Some of these channels are up to several tens of feet deep and may reach 61 m (200 ft) deep in the Zion National Park area. A regolith (thin, poorly-developed soil) formed over the topographic high areas between the channels (Biek et al. 2000).

Fossilized plants and animals in the Moenkopi are characteristic of a warm tropical setting that may have experienced monsoonal, wet-dry conditions (Stewart et al. 1972a; Dubiel 1994; Huntoon et al. 2000; Morris et al. 2000). Limestones and fossils in the Timpoweap, Virgin Limestone, and Shnabkaib Members of the Moenkopi Formation document transgressive episodes that spread marine environments into the region.

Reddish siltstone and sandstone record regressive events when the sea retreated to the west. Ripple marks, mudcracks, and thinly laminated bedding indicate that these interlayered red shale and siltstone units were deposited in tidal-flat and coastal-plain environments (Stewart et al. 1972a; Hamilton 1992; Biek et al. 2000).

The Early Triassic is separated from the Late Triassic by a regional unconformity. The unconformity marks a change from the shallow marine environments of the Lower Triassic Moenkopi Formation to mostly continental sedimentation in the Upper Triassic Chinle Formation. By this time, the Pipe Spring region was part of a large interior basin. Northerly flowing rivers deposited coarse sediments (Shinarump Conglomerate Member) in paleovalleys that eroded into the underlying Moenkopi Formation (Dubiel 1994; Biek et al. 2000). Meandering, high-sinuosity stream, flood plain, and lake sediments (Petrified Forest Member) overlay the coarse stream deposits.

Fossils of aquatic, crocodile-like phytosaurs, lungfish, snails, and lacustrine (lake) clams along with plant fossils of conifer trees, cycads, ferns, and horsetails indicate a lush, moist, coastal lowland environment in the Upper Triassic in what are now northern Arizona and southwestern Utah (Stewart et al. 1972b; Dubiel 1994; Biek et al. 2000). Periodically, volcanic ash drifted into the area from the west. Once deposited, it altered to the mineral bentonite. The crystalline structure of bentonite is unusual in that water can be absorbed into the structure, causing the mineral to expand when wet, and, upon drying, to shrink. This shrink and swell capacity causes bentonitic soil in the Moenkopi and Chinle Formations to become unstable, discourages plant growth, leads to erosion and mass wasting (a general term for any downslope transport of dislodged soil and rock material), and presents numerous difficulties when building roads and other structures.

Jurassic Period (199.6–145.5 million years ago)
During the Jurassic, the western active margin of North America was similar to today's western margin of South America, where eastward subduction of the seafloor gives rise to volcanism in the Andes Mountains. Volcanoes formed a north-south chain of mountains off the coast of western Pangaea, in what is now central Nevada. To the south, the landmass that would become

South America was splitting away from the Texas coast, just as Africa and Great Britain were rifting away from the present North American East Coast and opening up the Atlantic Ocean. The Ouachita Mountains, formed when South America collided with North America, remained a significant highland, and rivers from the highland flowed to the northwest, towards the Colorado Plateau. The Ancestral Rocky Mountains also remained topographically high during the Jurassic.

There is a gap of about ten million years between the Chinle Formation and the Early Jurassic Moenave Formation (the Moenave Formation is exposed north of the monument). The Moenave and Kayenta Formations were deposited in a variety of river, lake, and flood-plain environments (Biek et al. 2000). Studies of Jurassic current directions show that the Kayenta rivers flowed in a general westward to southwestward direction (Morris et al. 2000).

Mountains along the western active margin continued to rise in the Early Jurassic, as North America collided with the oceanic plate to the west. Eventually, a rain shadow was created, much like today's rain shadow in which the Sierra Nevada prevents moist Pacific air from reaching Nevada. Northern Arizona entered the arid, low-latitude (~11° north) climatic belt, and vast dune fields similar to the modern Sahara eventually overwhelmed the region (fig. 24).

These dune fields became the Navajo Sandstone, renowned for its uniformity and great thickness, which locally exceeds 610 m (2,000 ft). The Navajo was clearly the largest sand sea by volume ever known on Earth, and possibly the largest by area, as well. The characteristic high-angle cross-beds in the Navajo reach 18 m (60 ft) high and consist of moderately well-cemented, well-rounded, fine- to medium-grained quartz grains. Outcrops weather to bold, rounded cliffs. (Blakey 1994; Peterson 1994; Biek et al. 2000; Morris et al. 2000).

Cretaceous Period (145.5–65.5 million years ago)
The geologic strata above the Navajo Sandstone have been eroded from the Pipe Spring National Monument area. However, younger Jurassic and Cretaceous strata throughout the Colorado Plateau record multiple episodes of transgressions and regressions. Continued subduction along the west coast of North America initiated the Sevier Orogeny (about 75-105 mya), which thrust Paleozoic strata from west to east over younger, Mesozoic rocks. The Sevier Fault (fig. 4) separates the displaced, hanging wall strata from the geologic units in the footwall (fig. 6).

The Sevier Orogeny resulted in north-south trending mountain ranges that extended along the entire western margin of North America. The Pipe Spring National Monument area was part of this regional uplift. As the mountains rose, the Western Interior Province of North America began to subside. The Gulf of Mexico continued to rift open and marine water began to spill northward into the expanding Western Interior basin. At the same time, marine water began to advance onto the continent from the Arctic region.

The seas advanced and retreated many times during the Cretaceous until the most extensive interior seaway ever recorded drowned much of western North America (fig. 25). The Western Interior Seaway filled an elongate basin that extended from today's Gulf of Mexico to the Arctic Ocean, a distance of about 4,800 km (3,000 mi).

The onset of the Laramide Orogeny (beginning about 70 million years ago) was marked by a pronounced eastward shift in deformation throughout northern Arizona, Utah, and into Colorado. Unlike Sevier thrust faults, Laramide reverse faults cut deeply into Earth's crust, displacing Precambrian plutonic and metamorphic rocks to the surface. In contrast to Sevier thrust faults that dip at a low angle, generally 10-15°, relative to Earth's surface, Laramide reverse faults have steeply dipping fault planes at the surface that curve and die out in Precambrian basement crystalline rock at depths of up to 9 km (9,000 m) (5.7 mi or 30,000 ft) below sea level (Gries 1983; Erslev 1993).

During the Laramide Orogeny, tectonic forces folded and faulted Precambrian to Cretaceous age rocks into the Rocky Mountains and adjoining basins, but these compressive forces had seemingly little effect on the Colorado Plateau. The Colorado Plateau was primarily warped into broadly undulating convex (anticlinal) and concave (synclinal) folds and monoclines with very little large-scale faulting (Dickinson and Snyder 1978; Chapin and Cather 1983; Hamilton 1988; Erslev 1993). The Moccasin Monocline presents one example of a Laramide fold.

Paleogene and Neogene Periods (65.5–2.6 million years ago)

Explosive volcanism dominated the region to the west during Oligocene and early Miocene time (fig. 21) and probably inundated the Pipe Spring area with hundreds of feet of welded tuff that has since eroded away (Biek et al. 2000). Some of these enormous Mount St. Helens-type volcanoes may have produced eruptions that exceeded the largest Yellowstone eruptions (Dave Sharrow, hydrologist, National Park Service, written communication, 2005). About 21 million years ago, a type of mushroom-shaped igneous intrusion called a 'laccolith' formed between what are now St. George and Cedar City, Utah. Debris -flows carried boulders from this intrusion onto the Upper Kolob Plateau.

About 20 million years ago, during the Miocene Epoch, the tectonic regime along the southwestern margin of the United States changed when the North American Plate intersected the Pacific Plate (fig. 26). Transform faulting between the North American and Pacific Plates, and oblique convergence of the North American Plate with the Cocos Plate, began to pull apart, or extend, the crust beneath the southwestern United States—a process that eventually formed today's Basin-and-Range Province. While most of the Colorado Plateau was not greatly affected by Basin-and-Range normal faulting, extension

broke the western margin of the Colorado Plateau into a series of large blocks bounded by the north-south trending Hurricane, Sevier, Paunsaugunt, and other faults (fig. 4) (Gregory 1950; Biek et al. 2000). These large fault systems parallel the western margin of the Colorado Plateau. Pipe Spring National Monument, Zion National Park, Bryce Canyon National Park, and Cedar Breaks National Monument lie in a transition zone between the Colorado Plateau and the Basin-and-Range Province.

Quaternary Period (2.6 million years ago to present)

Exposures of Pleistocene (2.6 million to 11,700 years ago) alluvial fan deposits form stony surfaces along the base of the Vermilion Cliffs, northeast of Pipe Spring National Monument (Billingsley et al. 2004). Southeast of Pipe Spring National Monument, alluvial terrace-gravel deposits are scattered along the lower reaches of Bulrush Wash and Bitter Seeps Wash. These Pleistocene deposits range from 3 m (10 ft) to 15 m (50 ft) thick.

Pollen collected from Pleistocene deposits in the Southwest does not indicate any clear glacial/interglacial vegetation or climates prior to approximately 115,000 years ago, the onset of the Wisconsinan glacial stage (fig. 27) (Smiley et al. 1991). Vegetation patterns indicate a mild climate, similar to today's interglacial climate. During the Wisconsin glacial stage, about 115,000 to 10,000 years ago, climates were more varied and produced intense cyclonic storms and cold winters (Smiley et al. 1991). During the late Wisconsin (28,000–10,000 years ago), cool, dry summers on the Colorado Plateau contrasted with winters that had increased precipitation relative to today's climate (Patton et al. 1991).

Volcanic activity continued from the Tertiary into the Quaternary along the western margin of the Colorado Plateau (Luedke and Smith 1991; Patton et al. 1991). In the St. George, Utah, area, near Zion National Park, Quaternary eruptions may be less than 1,000 years old. During Pliocene through late Pleistocene, basaltic lava flows and pyroclastics erupted from vents in the Uinkaret volcanic field, north of the Colorado River in northwestern Arizona (Patton et al. 1991). The basaltic flows seem to be controlled by the north-trending extensional fault system.

Over the last several million years, minimum uplift rates relative to the adjacent Basin-and-Range Province have been about 26 meters per million years (m/my) (85 ft/my) in the Pipe Spring region. Large-scale mass wasting has accompanied the uplift of the Colorado Plateau. Landslides, like those at the base of the Vermillion Cliffs, are common along the escarpments that mark the various plateaus (Patton et al. 1991; Billingsley et al. 2004).

Holocene deposits in Pipe Spring National Monument are locally-derived from bedrock outcrops. These light-red, gray, and brown alluvial (stream) and eolian (wind) surficial sediments form deposits generally 1–18 m (3–60 ft) thick (Billingsley et al. 2004). The alluvial fans and alluvial terrace deposits derive from Triassic and Jurassic strata of the Vermilion Cliffs. Local fluvial deposits below the Vermilion Cliffs, and outcrops of the Navajo Sandstone on Moccasin and Moquith Mountains, provide the fine sediment for the eolian deposits. During wet climatic conditions, grassy vegetation stabilizes the eolian deposits, but during prolonged dry conditions, the eolian deposits again become active.

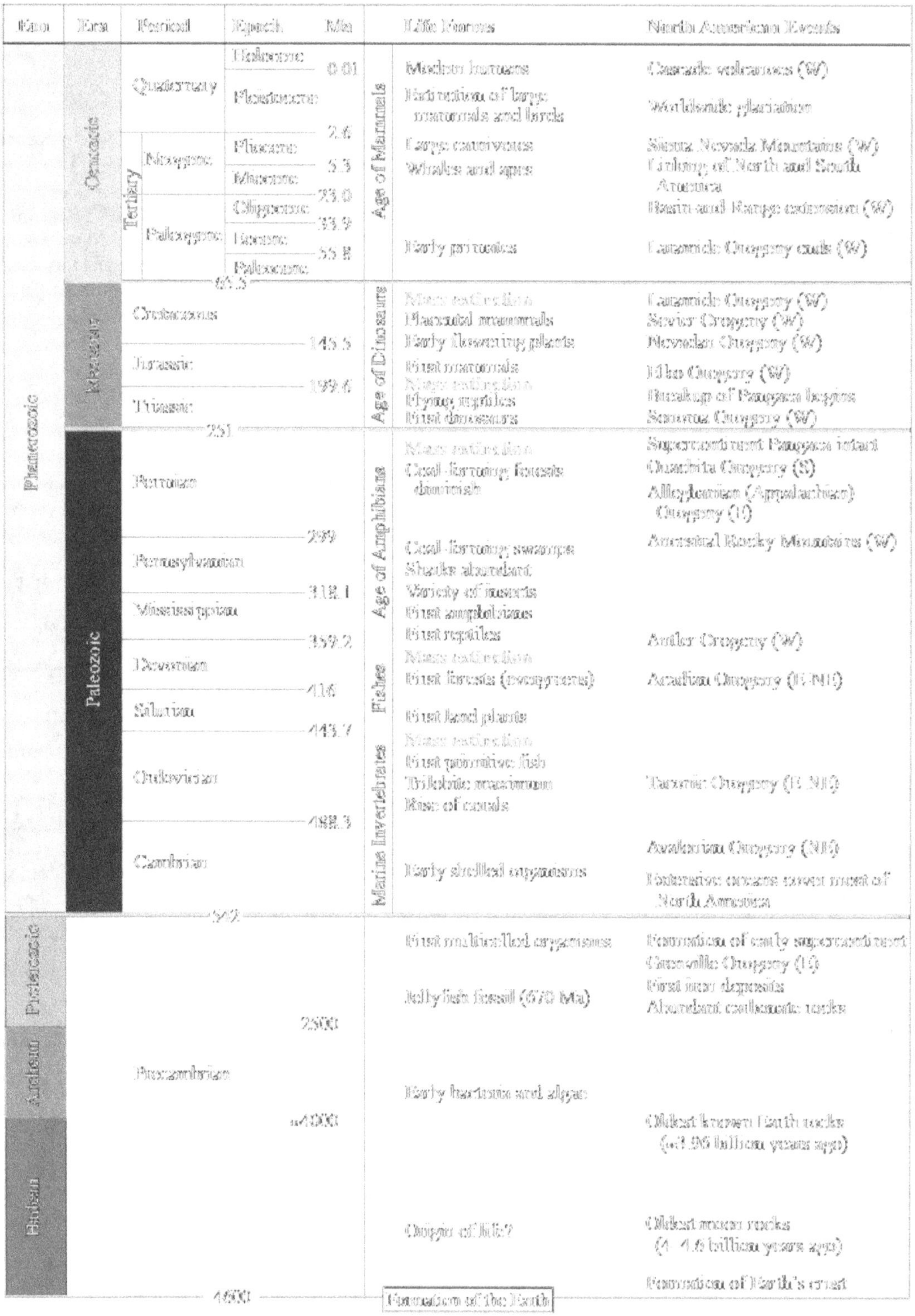

Figure 21. Geologic time scale. Geologic time scale. Included are major life history and tectonic events occurring on the North American continent. Red lines indicate major unconformities between eras. Isotopic ages shown are in millions of years (Ma). Compass directions in parentheses indicate the regional location of individual geologic events. Adapted from the U.S. Geological Survey, http://pubs.usgs.gov/fs/2007/3015/ with additional information from the International Commission on Stratigraphy. http://www.stratigraphy.org/view.php?id=25.

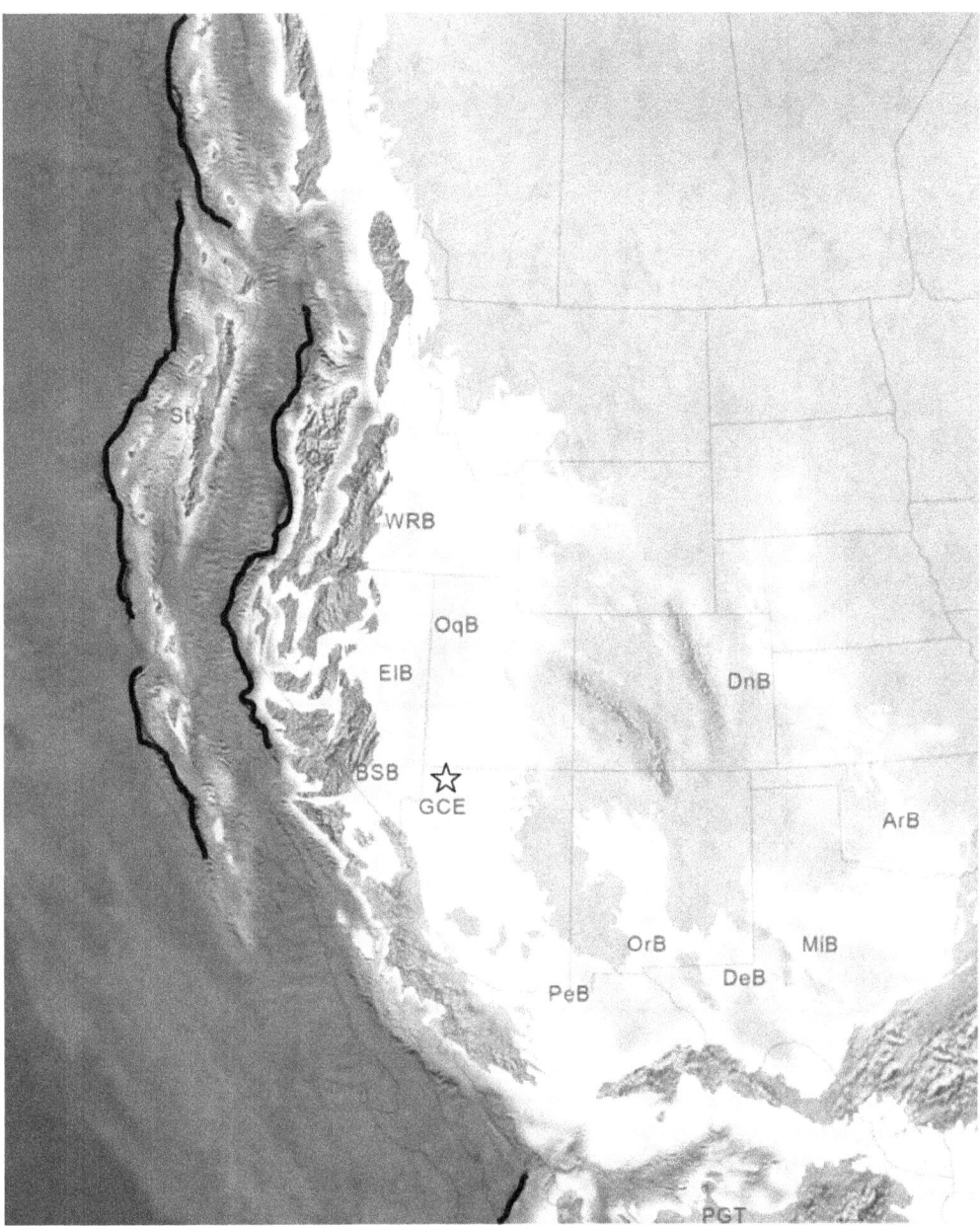

Figure 22. Early Permian paleogeographic map of the western United States during deposition of the Kaibab Formation. Approximately 270 million years ago, Arizona (yellow star) was located just north of the equator, as the global landmasses came together to form the supercontinent, Pangaea. Actively subsiding basins during this time include: Arbuckle (Anadarko) Basin (ArB), Bird Spring Basin (BSB), Delaware Basin (DeB), Denver Basin (DnB), Ely Basin (ElB), Grand Canyon Embayment (GCE), Midland Basin (MiB), Oquirrah Basin (OqB), Orogrande Basin (OrB), Pedregosa Basin (PeB), and Wood River Basin (WRB). Many of these basins became prolific oil and gas basins. Subduction zones (black lines) along the western margin of Pangaea would eventually accrete the following terranes to North America: Peri-Gondwanan terrane (PGT) to the south, Quesnell terrane (QT) in present-day Idaho, and Stikine terrane (St) in present-day western Washington. Yellow, orange, brown and gray colors are land areas, with dark brown representing higher elevations. Dark brown areas in Colorado are remnants of the Ancestral Rocky Mountains that formed when South America sutured onto North America in the Pennsylvanian Period. Blue colors represent water. Light blue areas represent shallower, near-shore environments. Map modified from Dr. Ron Blakey's (Northern Arizona University) paleogeographic map: http://jan.ucc.nau.edu/rcb7/garm270.jpg, accessed August 2009.

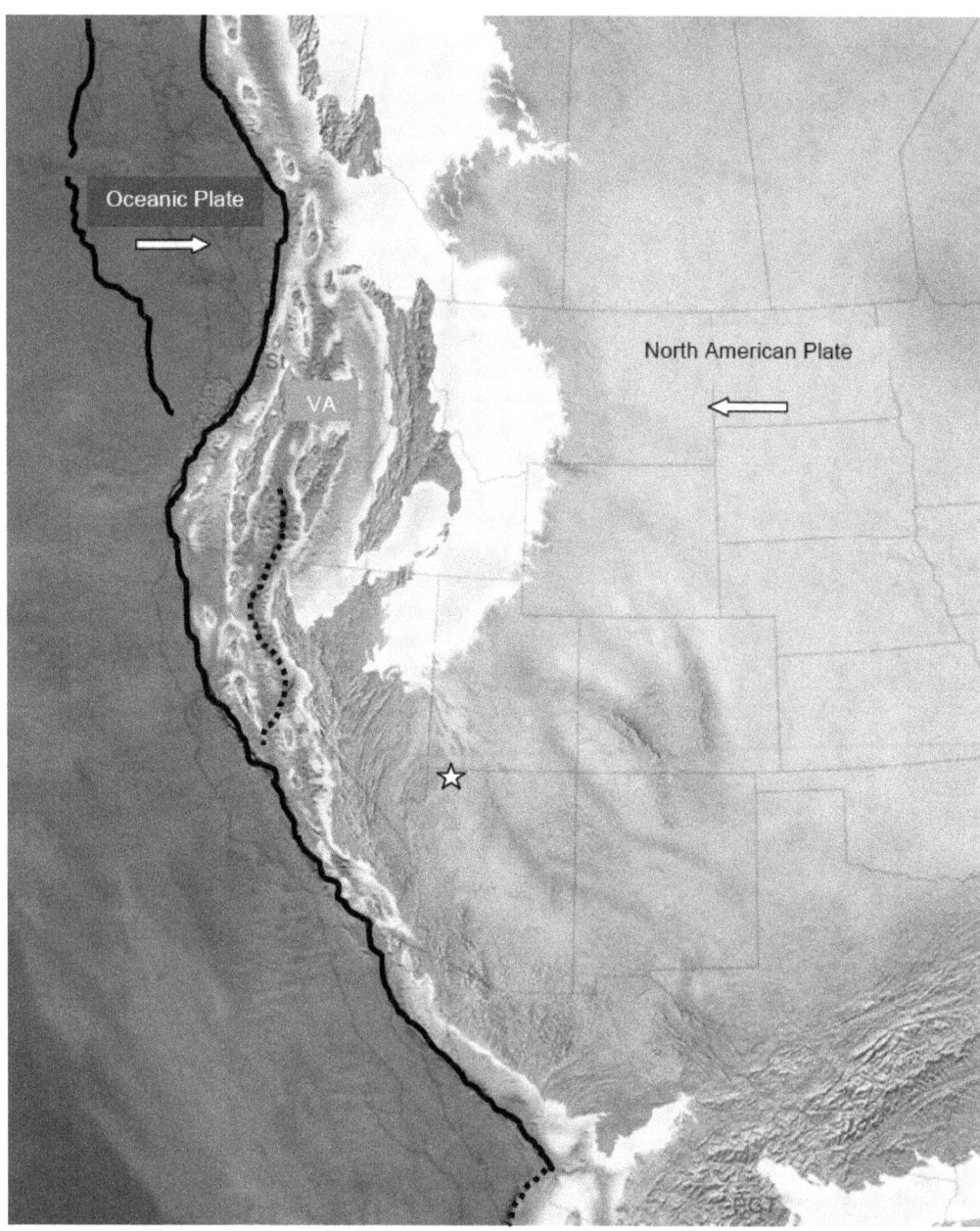

Figure 23. Early Triassic paleogeographic map of the western United States during deposition of the Moenkopi Formation. Approximately 240 million years ago, a broad fluvial and shallow marine depositional system covered much of Arizona, Utah, and Nevada. To the west, plate subduction and collision, marked by the solid and dashed black lines, resulted in the Sonoma Orogeny and the eventual accretion of volcanic arcs (VA) to the North American continent. Highlands in Colorado (dark brown) are remnants of the Ancestral Rocky Mountains. Yellow star represents the approximate location of today's Pipe Spring National Monument. Map modified from Dr. Ron Blakey's (Northern Arizona University) paleogeographic map: http://jan.ucc.nau.edu/rcb7/garm240.jpg, accessed August 2009.

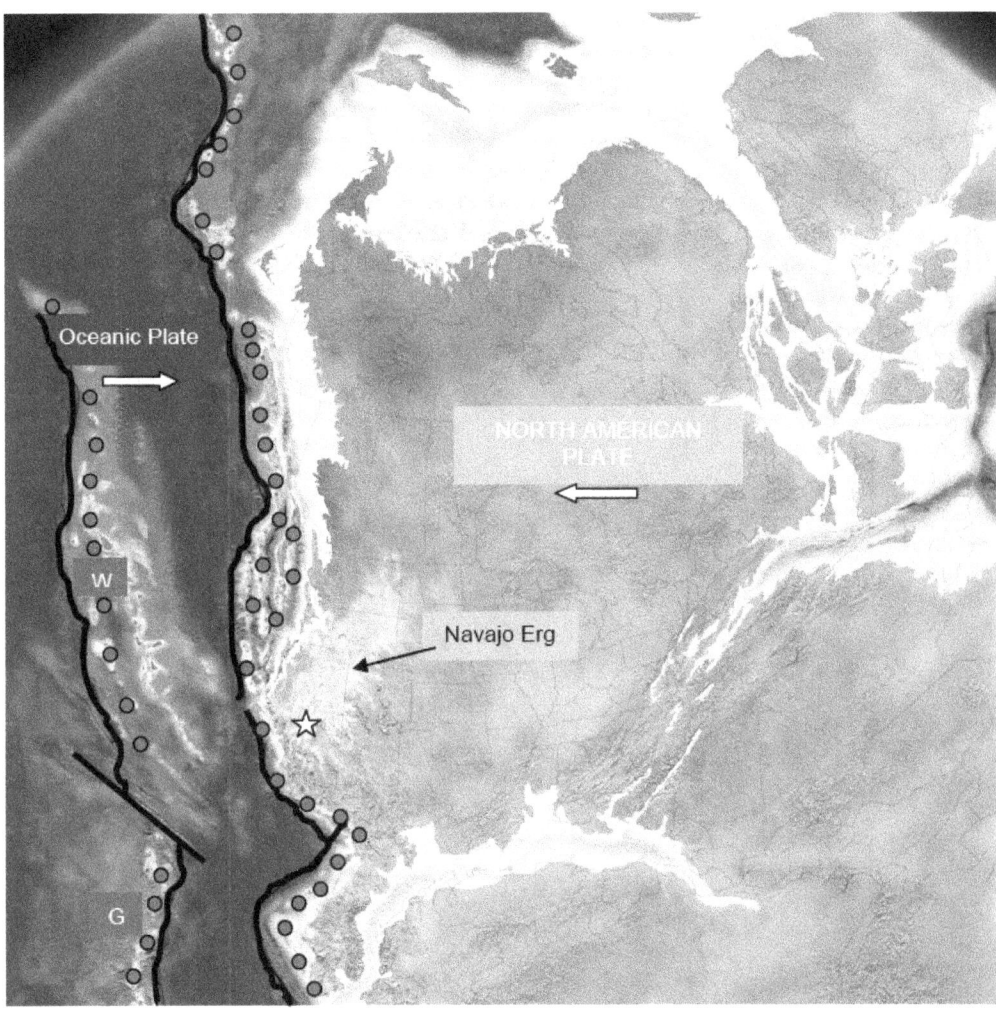

Figure 24. Early Jurassic paleogeographic map of North America during deposition of the Navajo Sandstone. Approximately 180 million years ago, the extensive Navajo sand sea (erg) spread across the western United States.) A few remnants of the Ancestral Rocky Mountains still remain topographically high in Colorado and northern New Mexico. Volcanic arcs (red dots) form above subduction zones (black lines). The superterrane Greater Wrangellia (W) and the Guerrero terrane (G) lie to the west. The yellow star represents the approximate location of today's Pipe Spring National Monument. Map modified from Dr. Ron Blakey's (Northern Arizona University), paleogeographic map: http://jan.ucc.nau.edu/rcb7/namJ180.jpg, accessed August 2009.

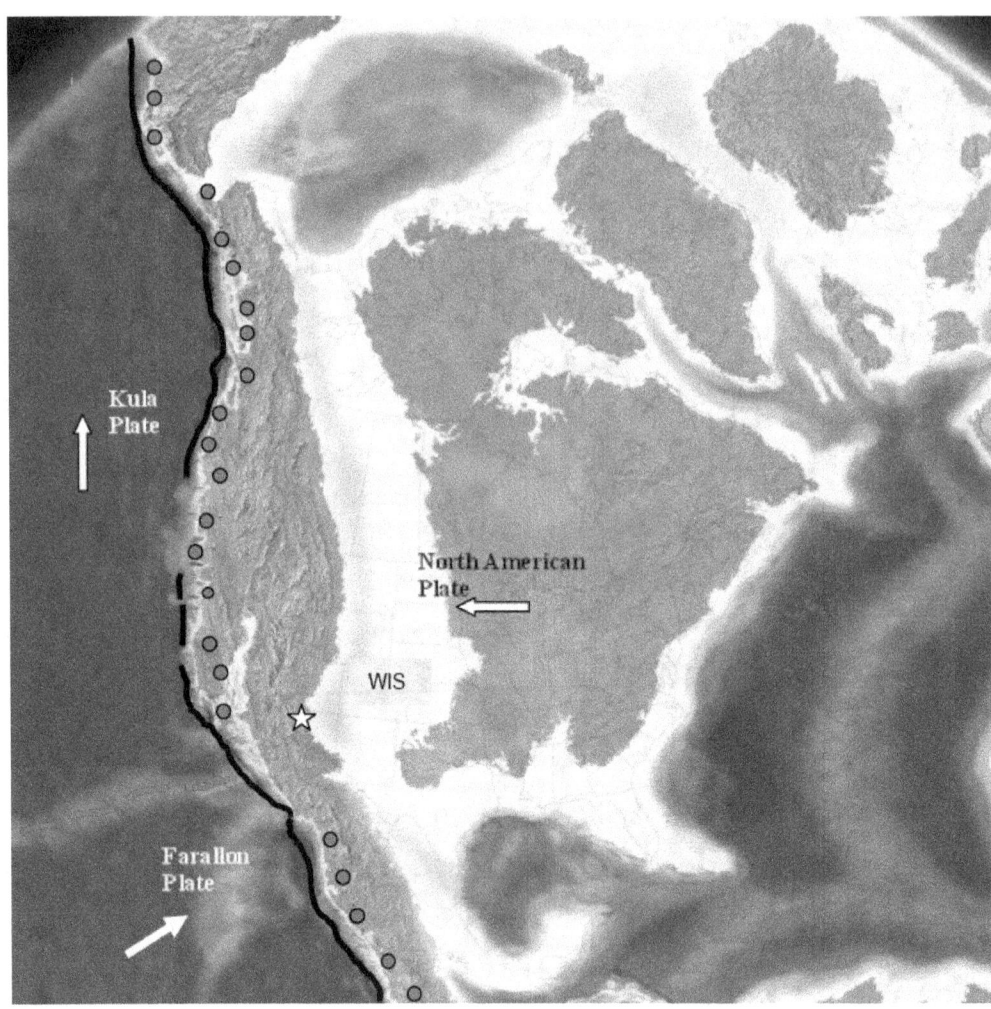

Figure 25. Cretaceous paleogeographic map of North America. Approximately 85 million years ago, the Western Interior Seaway (WIS) spread from the Gulf of Mexico to the Arctic Ocean. Volcanoes (red dots) erupted along the western margin of North America above an active subduction zone (black line). Lithospheric plate collision and subduction of the Kula and Farallon oceanic plates beneath North America resulted in the Sevier Orogeny and mountains rising in the west. The dashed red line represents the approximate border between the Farallon plate and the Kula plate. Northwestern Arizona (yellow star) is located along the western margin of the Western Interior Seaway. Map modified from Dr. Ron Blakey's (Northern Arizona University) paleogeographic map, http://jan.ucc.nau.edu/~rcb7/namK85.jpg, accessed August 2009.

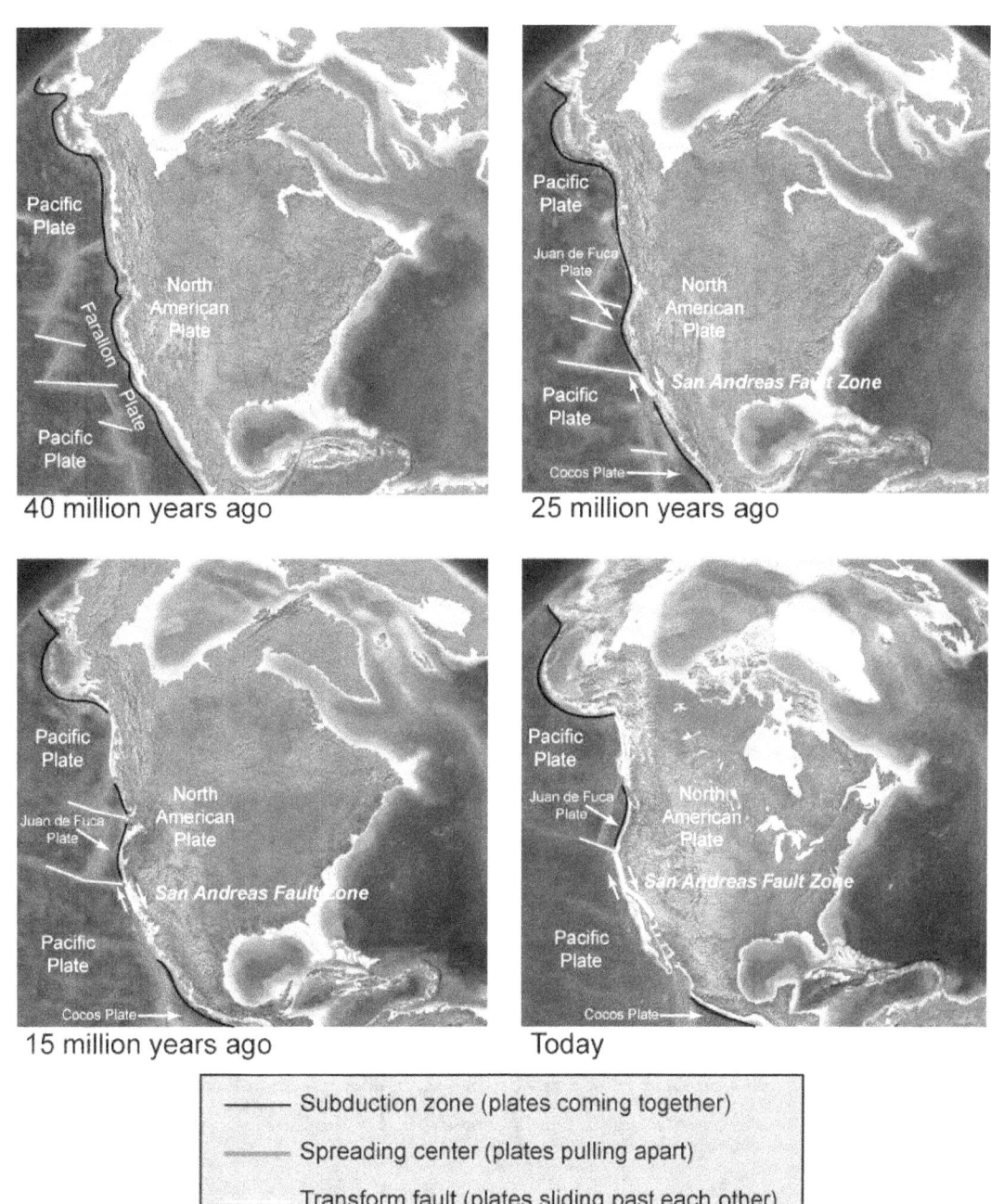

Figure 26. Plate tectonic evolution along the western margin of North America. Approximately 25 million years ago, the North American Plate intersected the Pacific Plate, initiating a transform (strike-slip) fault and the San Andreas fault zone (thick yellow line; relative plate motion indicated by yellow arrows). Oblique convergence and transform faulting began to pull apart, or extend, the crust under the southwestern United States and initiated Basin-and-Range style normal faulting. The trailing remnants of the subducting Farallon Plate are known as the Juan de Fuca and Cocos plates. Modified by Jason Kenworthy (NPS Geologic Resources Division) from Dr. Ron Blakey's (Northern Arizona University) paleogeographic maps: http://jan.ucc.nau.edu/~rcb7/nam.html, accessed January 2010.

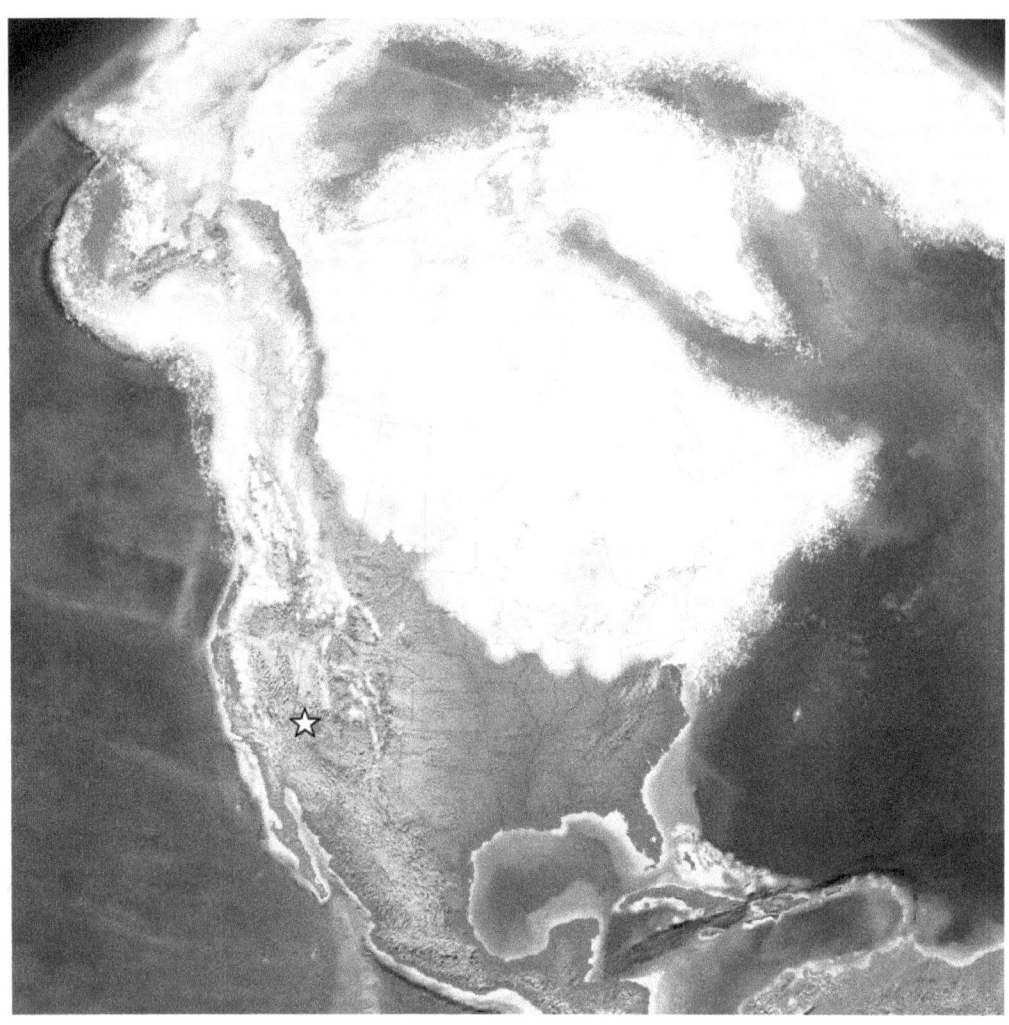

+ure 27. Pleistocene paleogeographic map at the onset of the Wisconsinan stage of the Pleistocene Ice Age. Approximately 126,000 years ago, lakes covered large areas of Utah and Nevada. The yellow star represents the approximate location of today's Pipe Spring National Monument. Brown is land; blue is water; white is ice and snow. Map modified from Dr. Ron Blakey's (Northern Arizona University) paleogeographic map: http://jan.ucc.nau.edu/~rcb7/namQ.jpg, accessed October 24, 2007.

Glossary

This glossary contains brief definitions of technical geologic terms used in this report. Not all geologic terms used are referenced. For more detailed definitions or to find terms not listed here please visit: http://geomaps.wr.usgs.gov/parks/misc/glossarya.html.

absolute age. The geologic age of a fossil, rock, feature, or event in years; commonly refers to radiometrically determined ages.

active margin. A continental margin where significant volcanic and earthquake activity occurs; commonly a convergent plate margin.

adit. A horizontal passage from the surface into a mine.

alluvium. Stream-deposited sediment.

aquifer. A rock or sedimentary unit that is sufficiently porous that it has a capacity to hold water, sufficiently permeable to allow water to move through it, and currently saturated to some level.

arc. See "island arc."

ash (volcanic). Fine pyroclastic material ejected from a volcano (also see "tuff").

basement. The undifferentiated rocks, commonly igneous and metamorphic, that underlie the rocks exposed at the surface.

bed. The smallest sedimentary strata unit, commonly ranging in thickness from one centimeter to a meter or two and distinguishable from beds above and below.

bedding. Depositional layering or stratification of sediments.

block (fault). A crustal unit bounded by faults, either completely or in part.

calcareous. Describes rock or sediment that contains calcium carbonate.

chert. A extremely hard sedimentary rock with conchoidal (smooth curved surface) fracturing. It consists chiefly of interlocking crystals of quartz (syn: flint).

clast. An individual grain or rock fragment in a sedimentary rock, produced by the physical disintegration of a larger rock mass.

clastic. Describes rock or sediment made of fragments of pre-existing rocks.

clay. Can be used to refer to clay minerals or as a sedimentary fragment size classification (less than 1/256 mm [0.00015 in]).

conglomerate. A coarse-grained, generally unsorted, sedimentary rock consisting of cemented rounded clasts larger than 2 mm (0.08 in).

continental crust. The crustal rocks rich in silica and alumina that underlie the continents; ranging in thickness from 35 km (22 mi) to 60 km (37 mi) under mountain ranges.

continental rise. The gently sloping region from the foot of the continental slope to the abyssal plain; it generally has smooth topography but may have submarine canyons.

continental shelf. The shallowly submerged part of a continental margin extending from the shoreline to the continental slope with water depths less than 200 m (660 ft).

continental shield. A continental block of Earth's crust that has remained relatively stable over a long period of time and has undergone only gentle warping compared to the intense deformation of bordering crust.

continental slope. The relatively steep slope from the outer edge of the continental shelf down to the more gently sloping ocean depths of the continental rise or abyssal plain.

convergent margin. An active boundary where two tectonic plates are colliding. See "active margin."

craton. The relatively old and geologically stable interior of a continent (also see "continental shield").

cross-bedding. Uniform to highly varied sets of inclined sedimentary beds deposited by wind or water that indicate distinctive flow conditions (e.g., direction and depth).

cross section. A graphical interpretation of geology, structure, and/or stratigraphy in the third (vertical) dimension based on mapped and measured geological extents and attitudes depicted in a vertically oriented plane.

crust. Earth's outermost compositional shell, 10 to 40 km (6 to 25 mi) thick, consisting predominantly of relatively low-density silicate minerals (also see "oceanic crust" and "continental crust").

cryptocrystalline. Describes the texture of a rock consisting of crystals that are too small to be recognized and separately distinguished even under the ordinary microscope.

cryptogamic soil. The brown crust on sandy, desert soils that is composed of an association of algae, lichen, mosses, and fungi and which helps stabilize the soil.

crystalline. Describes a regular, orderly, repeating geometric structural arrangement of atoms.

deformation. A general term for the process of faulting, folding, and shearing of rocks as a result of various Earth forces such as compression (pushing together) and extension (pulling apart).

desert pavement. A natural residual concentration of wind-polished, closely packed pebbles, boulders, and other rock fragments, mantling a desert surface where wind action and sheetwash have removed all smaller particles, and usually protecting the underlying finer-grained material from further erosion. Also called 'desert armor.'

dip. The angle between a structural surface and a horizontal reference plane measured normal to their line of intersection.

dip-slip fault. A fault with measurable offset where the relative movement is parallel to the dip of the fault.

dolomite. A carbonate sedimentary rock of which more than 50% by weight or by areal percentages under the microscope consists of the mineral dolomite (calcium-magnesium carbonate: $CaMg(CO_3)_2$).

dolomitic. Describes a dolomite-bearing rock, or a rock containing dolomite.

dune. A low mound or ridge of sediment, usually sand, deposited by wind.

electrical resistivity survey. A measure of the difficulty with which electric current flows through unconsolidated sediment and rock.

electromagnetic survey (method). An electrical exploration method based on the measurement of alternating magnetic fields associated with currents artificially or naturally maintained in the subsurface.

eolian. Formed, eroded, or deposited by or related to the action of the wind.

evaporite. A sedimentary rock composed primarily of minerals produced from a saline solution as a result of extensive or total evaporation of the solvent (usually water).

extension. In structural geology, a strain term signifying increase in length. Opposite of compression (see "pull-apart basin").

fault. A break in rock along which relative movement occurs between the two sides.

footwall. The mass of rock beneath a fault surface (see "hanging wall").

formation. Fundamental rock-stratigraphic unit that is mappable, lithologically distinct from adjoining strata, and has definable upper and lower contacts.

fracture. Irregular breakage of a mineral; also any break in a rock (e.g., crack, joint, or fault).

graben. A down-dropped structural block bounded by steeply dipping, normal faults (see "horst").

gypsiferous. Gypsum-bearing.

gypsum. The most common sulfate mineral (calcium sulfate). Frequently associated with halite and anhydrite in evaporites.

hanging wall. The mass of rock above a fault surface (see "footwall").

horst. Areas of relative "up" between grabens, representing the geologic surface left behind as grabens drop. The best example is the Basin-and-Range province of Nevada. The basins are grabens and the ranges are weathered horsts. Grabens become a locus for sedimentary deposition.

igneous. Refers to a rock or mineral that originated from molten material; one of the three main classes or rocks—igneous, metamorphic, and sedimentary.

intrusion. A body of igneous rock that invades (pushes into) older rock. The invading rock may be a plastic solid or magma.

island arc. A line or arc of volcanic islands formed over and parallel to a subduction zone.

joint. A semi-planar break in rock without relative movement of rocks on either side of the fracture surface.

karst topography. Topography characterized by abundant sinkholes and caverns formed by the dissolution of calcareous rocks.

laccolith. A mushroom- or arcuate-shaped pluton that has intruded sedimentary strata and domed up the overlying sedimentary layers. Common on the Colorado Plateau.

lacustrine. Pertaining to, produced by, or inhabiting a lake or lakes.

lag gravel. A residual accumulation of coarse material remaining on a surface after the finer material has been blown away by winds.

landslide. Any process or landform resulting from rapid, gravity-driven mass movement.

lava. Still-molten or solidified magma that has been extruded onto Earth's surface though a volcano or fissure.

lens. A sedimentary deposit characterized by converging surfaces, thick in the middle and thinning out toward the edges, resembling a convex lens.

lithification. The conversion of sediment into solid rock.

lithology. The physical description or classification of a rock or rock unit based on characters such as its color, mineral composition, and grain size.

lithosphere. The relatively rigid outmost shell of Earth's structure, 50 to 100 km (31 to 62 miles) thick, that encompasses the crust and uppermost mantle.

magma. Molten rock beneath Earth's surface capable of intrusion and extrusion.

mantle. The zone of Earth's interior between the crust and core.

marker bed. A key layer used to trace a geologic unit from one geographic location to another.

mass wasting. A general term for any downslope transport of dislodged soil and rock material, such as a landslide or slump.

matrix. The fine grained material between coarse (larger) grains in igneous rocks or poorly sorted clastic sediments or rocks. Also refers to rock or sediment in which a fossil is embedded.

member. A lithostratigraphic unit with definable contacts; a member subdivides a formation.

mesa. A broad, flat-topped erosional hill or mountain bounded by steeply sloping sides or cliffs.

meta–. A prefix used with the name of a sedimentary or igneous rock, indicating that the rock has been metamorphosed.

metamorphic. Describes the process of metamorphism or its results. One of the three main classes of rocks—igneous, metamorphic, and sedimentary.

metamorphism. Literally, a change in form. Metamorphism occurs in rocks through mineral alteration, genesis, and/or recrystallization from increased heat and pressure.

monocline. A one-limbed flexure in strata that is usually flat lying except in the flexure itself.

mudcracks. Cracks formed in clay, silt, or mud by shrinkage during subaerial dehydration.

normal fault. A dip-slip fault in which the hanging wall moves down relative to the footwall.

oceanic crust. Earth's crust formed at spreading ridges that underlies the ocean basins. Oceanic crust is 6 to 7 km (3 to 4 miles) thick and generally of basaltic composition.

orogeny. A mountain-building event.

outcrop. Any part of a rock mass or formation that is exposed or "crops out" at Earth's surface.

paleogeography. The study, description, and reconstruction of the physical landscape from past geologic periods.

Pangaea. A theoretical, single supercontinent that existed during the Permian and Triassic periods.

permeability. A measure of the relative ease with which fluids move through the pore spaces of rocks or sediments.

plateau. A broad, flat-topped topographic high (both terrestrial and marine) of great extent and elevation above the surrounding plains, canyons, or valleys.

plate tectonics. The concept that the lithosphere is broken up into a series of rigid plates that move over Earth's surface above a more fluid asthenosphere.

pluton (plutonic). A body of intrusive igneous rock that crystallized at some depth beneath Earth's surface.

point bar. Ridges of sand and gravel developed on the inside of a stream's growing meander bend where the river's energy decreases and sediment is deposited.

porosity. The proportion of void space (e.g., pores or voids) in a volume of rock or sediment deposit.

pull-apart basin. A topographic depression created by an extensional bend or extensional overstep along a strike-slip fault.

pyroclastic. Describes clastic rock material formed by volcanic explosion or aerial expulsion from a volcanic vent; also pertaining to rock texture of explosive origin. In the plural, the term is used as a noun.

quartzite. Metamorphosed quartz sandstone.

radiometric age. An age expressed in years and calculated from the quantitative determination of radioactive elements and their decay products.

recharge. Infiltration processes that replenish groundwater.

reflection survey. Record of the time it takes for seismic waves generated from a controlled source to return to the surface. Used to interpret the depth to the subsurface feature that generated the reflections.

refraction survey. A type of seismic survey that measures the travel times of seismic waves that have travelled nearly parallel through a medium of high-velocity. Used to determine general soil types, the depth to strata boundaries, or depth to bedrock.

regression. A long-term seaward retreat of the shoreline or relative fall of sea level.

resistivity. See "electrical resistivity survey."

reverse fault. A contractional high-angle (greater than 45°) dip-slip fault in which the hanging wall moves up relative to the footwall (also see "thrust fault").

ripple marks. The undulating, subparallel, usually small-scale ridge pattern formed on sediment by the flow of wind or water.

rip-up clast. A mud clast (usually of flat shape) that has been "ripped up" by currents from a semiconsolidated mud deposit, transported, and deposited elsewhere.

sabkha. A coastal environment in an arid climate where evaporation rates are high.

sand. A clastic particle smaller than a granule and larger than a silt grain, having a diameter in the range of 1/16 mm (0.0025 in) to 2 mm (0.08 in).

sand sheet. A large irregularly shaped plain of eolian sand, lacking the discernible slip faces that are common on dunes.

sandstone. Clastic sedimentary rock of predominantly sand-sized grains.

scarp. A steep cliff or topographic step resulting from displacement on a fault, or by mass movement, or erosion. Also called an "escarpment."

sediment. An eroded and deposited, unconsolidated accumulation of rock and mineral fragments.

sedimentary rock. A consolidated and lithified rock consisting of clastic and/or chemical sediment(s). One of the three main classes of rocks—igneous, metamorphic, and sedimentary.

seismic reflection. See "reflection survey."

seismic refraction. See "refraction survey."

shale. A clastic sedimentary rock made of clay-sized particles that exhibit parallel splitting properties.

sheetwash (sheet erosion). The removal of thin layers of surface material more or less evenly from an extensive area of gently sloping land by broad continuous sheets of running water rather than by streams flowing in well-defined channels.

silt. Clastic sedimentary material intermediate in size between fine-grained sand and coarse clay (1/256 to 1/16 mm [0.00015 to 0.002 in]).

siltstone. A variably lithified sedimentary rock composed of silt-sized grains.

spring. A site where water issues from the surface due to the intersection of the water table with the ground surface.

strata. Tabular or sheet-like masses or distinct layers of rock.

strike-slip fault. A fault with measurable offset where the relative movement is parallel to the strike of the fault. Said to be "sinistral" (left-lateral) if relative motion of the block opposite the observer appears to be to the left. "Dextral" (right-lateral) describes relative motion to the right.

structure. The attitude and relative positions of the rock masses of an area resulting from such processes as faulting, folding, and igneous intrusions.

subduction zone. A convergent plate boundary where oceanic lithosphere descends beneath a continental or oceanic plate and is carried down into the mantle.

syncline. A downward curving (concave up) fold with layers that dip inward; the core of the syncline contains the stratigraphically-younger rocks.

talus. Rock fragments, usually coarse and angular, lying at the base of a cliff or steep slope from which they have been derived.

tectonic. Relating to large-scale movement and deformation of Earth's crust.

terrace (stream). Step-like benches surrounding the present floodplain of a stream due to dissection of previous flood plain(s), stream bed(s), and/or valley floor(s).

terrane. A large region or group of rocks with similar geology, age, or structural style.

terrestrial. Relating to land, Earth, or its inhabitants.

thrust fault. A contractional dip-slip fault with a shallowly dipping fault surface (less than 45°) where the hanging wall moves up and over relative to the footwall.

topography. The general morphology of Earth's surface, including relief and locations of natural and anthropogenic features.

transgression. Landward migration of the sea as a result of a relative rise in sea level.

trend. The direction or azimuth of elongation of a linear geologic feature.

tuff. Generally fine-grained, igneous rock formed of consolidated volcanic ash.

type locality. The geographic location where a stratigraphic unit (or fossil) is well displayed, formally defined, and derives its name. The place of original description.

unconformity. An erosional or non-depositional surface bounded on one or both sides by sedimentary strata that marks a period of missing time.

uplift. A structurally high area in the crust, produced by movement that raises the rocks.

volcanic. Related to volcanoes. Igneous rock crystallized at or near the Earth's surface (e.g., lava).

water table. The upper surface of the saturated zone; the zone of rock in an aquifer saturated with water.

weathering. The set of physical, chemical, and biological processes by which rock is broken down.

References

This section lists references cited in this report. A more complete geologic bibliography is available from the National Park Service Geologic Resources Division.

Bagley, W. 2002. Pipe Springs legends will keep flowing. *Salt Lake Tribune*, B1. March 24, 2002.

Barrett, D. C., and O. R. Williams. 1986. *An evaluation of the decline in spring flow at Pipe Spring National Monument.* Memo report to the Chief, Water Rights Branch.

Becker, L., R.J. Poreda, A.G. Hunt, T.E. Bunch, and M. Rampino. 2001. Impact event at the Permian-Triassic boundary: Evidence from extraterrestrial noble gases in fullerenes. *Science* (February 23): 1530-1533.

Biek, R. F., G. C. Willis, M. D. Hylland, and H. H. Doelling. 2000. Geology of Zion National Park, Utah. In *Geology of Utah's parks and monuments*, ed. D. A. Sprinkel, T. C. Chidsey Jr., and P. B. Anderson, 107-138. Utah Geological Association Publication 28.

Billingsley, G. H., S. S. Priest, and T. J. Felger. 2004. *Geologic map of Pipe Spring National Monument and the western Kaibab-Paiute Indian Reservation, Mohave County, Arizona.* Scale 1:31,680. U.S. Geological Survey, Scientific Investigation Map 2863. http://pubs.er.usgs.gov/usgspubs/sim/sim2863.

Blakey, R. C. 1994. Paleogeographic and tectonic controls on some Lower and Middle Jurassic erg deposits, Colorado Plateau. In *Mesozoic systems of the Rocky Mountain region, USA*, ed. M. V. Caputo, J. A. Peterson, and K. J. Franczyk, 273-298. Society for Sedimentary Geology, Rocky Mountain Section.

Chapin, C. E., and S.M. Cather. 1983. Eocene tectonics and sedimentation in the Colorado Plateau – Rocky Mountain area. In *Rocky Mountain foreland basins and uplifts*, ed. J. Lowell, 33-56. Rocky Mountain Association of Geologists.

Christiansen, E. II, B.J. Kowallis, and M.D. Barton. 1994. Temporal and spatial distribution of volcanic ash in Mesozoic sedimentary rocks of the Western Interior: An alternative record of Mesozoic magmatism. In *Mesozoic systems of the Rocky Mountain region, USA*, ed. M. V. Caputo, J. A. Peterson, and K. J. Franczyk, 73-94. Society for Sedimentary Geology, Rocky Mountain Section.

Cuffey, R. J., M. J. Di Nardo-Magilton, and B. J. Herzing. 1998. Dinosaur footprints in the basal Navajo Sandstone (Lower Jurassic) at Pipe Spring National Monument, northwestern Arizona. In *The third National Park Service paleontological research volume*, ed. V. L. Santucci and L. McClelland, 149-152. Geologic Resources Division Technical Report NPS/NRGRD/GRDTR-98/01. Lakewood, CO: National Park Service.

http://www.nature.nps.gov/geology/paleontology/pub/grd3_3/pisp1.htm.

Dickinson, W. R., and W.S. Snyder. 1978. Plate tectonics of the Laramide Orogeny. In *Laramide folding associated with basement block faulting in the western United States*, ed. V. Matthews III, 355-366. Memoir 151. Boulder, CO: Geological Society of America.

Doelling, H. H. 2000. Geology of Arches National Park, Grand County, Utah. In *Geology of Utah's parks and monuments*, ed. D. A. Sprinkel, T. C. Chidsey Jr., and P. B. Anderson, 11-36. Utah Geological Association, Publication 28.

Dubiel, R. F. 1994. Triassic deposystems, paleogeography, and paleoclimate of the Western Interior. In *Mesozoic systems of the Rocky Mountain region, USA*, ed. M. V. Caputo, J. A. Peterson, and K. J. Franczyk, 133-168. Society for Sedimentary Geology, Rocky Mountain Section.

Erslev, E. A. 1993. Thrusts, back-thrusts, and detachment of Rocky Mountain foreland arches. In *Laramide basement deformation in the Rocky Mountain foreland of the western United States*, ed. C. J. Schmidt, R. B. Chase, and E. A. Erslev, 339-358. Special Paper 280. Boulder, CO: Geological Society of America.

Fenton, C. R., R. H. Webb, P. A. Pearthree, T. E. Cerling, and R. J. Poreda. 2001. Displacement rates on the Toroweap and Hurricane faults: Implications for Quaternary downcutting in the Grand Canyon, Arizona. *Geology* 29 (11): 1035-1038.

Gregory, H.E. 1950, *Geology and Geography of the Zion Park Region Utah and Arizona.* Professional Paper 220. Reston, VA: U.S. Geological Survey. http://pubs.er.usgs.gov/usgspubs/pp/pp220

Gries, R. 1983. North-south compression of Rocky Mountain foreland structures. In *Rocky Mountain foreland basins and uplifts*, ed. J. D. Lowell and R. Gries, 9-32. Rocky Mountain Association of Geologists.

Hamilton, W. B. 1988. *Laramide crustal shortening.* Memoir 171. Boulder, CO: Geological Society of America.

Hamilton, W. L. 1992. *The sculpturing of Zion.* Revised 1984 ed. Springdale, UT: Zion Natural History Association.

Huntoon, J. E., J. D. Stanesco, R. F. Dubiel, and J. Dougan. 2000. Geology of Natural Bridges National Monument, Utah, In *Geology of Utah's parks and monuments*, ed. D. A. Sprinkel, T. C. Chidsey Jr., and P. B. Anderson, 233-250. Utah Geological Association Publication 28.

Huntoon, P. W. 2003. Post-Precambrian tectonism in the Grand Canyon region. In *Grand Canyon geology*, ed. S. S. Beus and M. Morales, 222-259. 2nd ed. Oxford University Press.

Inglis, R. 1990. Water resources data of the Pipe Spring National Monument area, Arizona, 1977-1989. Water Resources Division Technical Report NPS/WRD/NRTR-90/02. Fort Collins, CO: National Park Service.

Inglis, R. 1997. *Monitoring and analysis of spring flows at Pipe Spring National Monument, Mojave County, Arizona.* Water Resources Division Technical Report NPS/NRWRD/NRTR-97/125. Fort Collins, CO: National Park Service. http://www.nature.nps.gov/water/technicalReports/ Intermountain/PISP_1997.pdf

Lawton, T. F. 1994. Tectonic setting of Mesozoic sedimentary basins, Rocky Mountain region, United States. In *Mesozoic systems of the Rocky Mountain region, USA*, ed. M. V. Caputo, J. A. Peterson, and K. J. Franczyk, 1-26. Society for Sedimentary Geology, Rocky Mountain Section.

Lockley, M. G. and A. P. Hunt. 1994. A review of Mesozoic vertebrate ichnofaunas of the Western Interior United States: Evidence and implications of a superior track record. In *Mesozoic systems of the Rocky Mountain region*, ed. M.V. Caputo, J.A. Peterson, and K.J. Franczyk, 95-103. Society for Sedimentary Geology, Rocky Mountain Section.

Luedke, R. G., and R. L. Smith. 1991. Quaternary volcanism in the western conterminous United States. In *Quaternary nonglacial geology: Conterminous U.S.*, ed. R. B. Morrison, 75-92. Geological Society of America, The Geology of North America K-2.

Lund, W. R., T. R. Knudsen, and G. S. Vice. 2008. *Paleoseismic reconnaissance of the Sevier Fault, Kane and Garfield Counties, Utah.* Paleoseismology of Utah 16, Special Study 122. Salt Lake City, UT: Utah Geological Survey.

Lund, W. R., W. J. Taylor, P. A. Pearthree, H. Stenner, L. Amoroso, and H. Hurlow. 2002. *Structural development and paleoseismicity of the Hurricane Fault, southwestern Utah and northwestern Arizona.* Fieldtrip Guidebook 2002 Rocky Mountain Section Annual Meeting. Cedar City, UT: Geological Society of America. http://geopubs.wr.usgs.gov/open-file/of02-172/chapters/chap1.pdf.

Martin, L. 2007. *Summary of spring flow decline and local hydrogeologic studies, 1969-2007, Pipe Spring National Monument.* Water Resources Division, Natural Resources Report NPS/NRPC/WRD/NRTR-

2007/365. Fort Collins, CO: National Park Service. http://www.nature.nps.gov/water/technicalReports/ Intermountain/PISP_Hydrology_Report.pdf

Mayerle, C. and S. Urquhart. 2008. *CSAMT geophysical survey, Pipe Springs project, Kanab, Utah.* Report Prepared for National Park Service, May 2008. Tucson, AZ: Zonge Engineering & Research Organization Inc.

McKoy, K. L. 2000. *Cultures at a crossroads: An administrative history of Pipe Spring National Monument.* Cultural Resources Selections 15. Denver, CO: National Park Service, Intermountain Region. http://www.nps.gov/pisp/historyculture/upload/PISP_ adhi.pdf.

Morris, T. H., V. W. Manning, and S. M. Ritter. 2000. Geology of Capitol Reef National Park, Utah. In *Geology of Utah's parks and monuments*, ed. D. A. Sprinkel, T. C. Chidsey Jr., and P. B. Anderson, 85-106. Utah Geological Association Publication 28.

National Park Service. 2004. *Pipe Spring National Monument. NCPN Phase III Report, Appendix E.* http://www.nature.nps.gov/im/units/ncpn/ link_library/park_descriptions/pisp_description.pdf.

Patton, P. C., N. Biggar, C. D. Condit, M. L. Gillam, D. W. Love, M. N. Machette, L. Mayer, R. B. Morrison, and J. N. Rosholt. 1991. Quaternary geology of the Colorado Plateau. In *Quaternary nonglacial geology: Conterminous U.S.*, ed. R. B. Morrison, 373-407. Geological Society of America, The Geology of North America K-2.

Peterson, F. 1994. Sand dunes, sabkhas, stream, and shallow seas: Jurassic paleogeography in the southern part of the Western Interior Basin. In *Mesozoic systems of the Rocky Mountain region, USA*, ed. M. V. Caputo, J. A. Peterson, and K. J. Franczyk, 233-272. Society for Sedimentary Geology, Rocky Mountain Section.

Peterson, J. A. 1980. Permian paleogeography and sedimentary provinces, west central United States. In *Paleozoic paleogeography of the west-central United States*, ed. T. D. Fouch and E. R. Magathan, 271-292. Society for Sedimentary Geology, Rocky Mountain Section.

Raup, D. M. 1991. *Extinction: Bad genes or bad luck?* New York: W.W. Norton and Company.

Rawson, R.R. and C.E. Turner-Peterson. 1980. Paleogeography of northern Arizona during the deposition of the Permian Toroweap Formation. In *Paleozoic paleogeography of the west-central United State*, ed. T.D. Fouch and E.R. Magathan, 341-352. Society for Sedimentary Geology, Rocky Mountain Section.

Rymer, M. J., R. D. Catchings, M. R. Goldman, C. E. Steedman, and G. Gandhok. 2007. *Subsurface structure of the Sevier Fault near Pipe Spring National Monument and the western Kaibab-Paiute Reservation, Mohave County, Arizona – A seismic reflection and refraction study.* Open-File Report (draft). Lakewood, CO: U.S. Geological Survey.

Sabol, T. A. 2005. Delineation of wellhead and springhead protection areas for the Kaibab Paiute Indian Reservation, Arizona. MS thesis, Northern Arizona University.

Santucci, V. L., A. P. Hunt, and M. G. Lockley. 1998. Fossil vertebrate tracks in National Park Service areas. *Dakoterra* 5: 107-114.

Santucci, V. L., J. P. Kenworthy, and A. L. Mims. 2009. Monitoring in situ paleontological resources. In *Geological Monitoring*, eds. R. Young and L. Norby, 189-204. Boulder, CO: Geological Society of America.

Sharrow, D. 2009. Physical resources information and issues overview report: Pipe Spring National Monument. Water Resources Division, Natural Resource Report NPS/NRPC/WRD/NRR—2009/149. Fort Collins, CO: National Park Service.

Silberling, N. J. and R.J. Roberts. 1962. *Pre-Tertiary stratigraphy and structure of northwestern Nevada.* Special Paper 72. Boulder, CO: Geological Society of America.

Smiley, T. L., R. A. Bryson, J. E. King, G. J. Kukla, and G. I. Smith. 1991. Quaternary paleoclimates. In *Quaternary nonglacial geology: Conterminous U.S.*, ed.

Roger B. Morrison, 13-45. Geological Society of America, The Geology of North America K-2.

Stewart, J. H., F. G. Poole, and R.F. Wilson. 1972A. *Stratigraphy and origin of the Triassic Moenkopi Formation and related strata in the Colorado Plateau region with a section on sedimentary petrology by R.A. Cadigan.* Professional Paper 691. Lakewood, CO: U.S. Geological Survey.

Stewart, J. H., F. G. Poole, and R.F. Wilson. 1972B. *Stratigraphy and origin of the Chinle Formation and related Upper Triassic strata in the Colorado Plateau region with a section on sedimentary petrology by R.A. Cadigan and on Conglomerate Studies by W. Thordarson, H.F. Albee, and J.H. Stewart.* Professional Paper 690. Lakewood, CO: U.S. Geological Survey.

Stokes, W.L. 1988. Dinosaur tour book. Salt Lake City: Starstone Publishing.

Truini, M. 1999. *Geohydrology of Pipe Spring National Monument area, northern Arizona.* Water-Resources Investigations Report 98-4263. Reston, VA: U.S. Geological Survey.

Truini, M., J.B. Fleming, and H.A. Pierce. 2004. *Preliminary investigation of structural controls of ground-water movement in Pipe Spring National Monument, Arizona.* Scientific Investigations Report 2004-5082. Reston, VA: U.S. Geological Survey. http://pubs.er.usgs.gov/usgspubs/sir/sir20045082.

Appendix A: Geologic Map Graphic

The following page is a snapshot of the geologic map for Pipe Spring National Monument. For a poster-size PDF of this map or for digital geologic map data, please see the included CD or visit the Geologic Resources Inventory publications Web page (http://www.nature.nps.gov/geology/inventory/gre_publications.cfm).

Appendix B: Scoping Summary

The following excerpts are from the GRI scoping summary for Pipe Spring National Monument. The contact information and Web addresses in this appendix may be outdated. Please contact the Geologic Resources Division for current information.

Summary

A geologic resources inventory workshop was held for Pipe Spring National Monument (PISP) on June 28, 2001 to discuss the park's geologic resources, to address the status of geologic mapping for compiling both paper and digital maps, and to assess resource management issues and needs. Cooperators from the NPS Geologic Resources Division (GRD), NPS Pipe Spring NM, Colorado State University (CSU), and United States Geologic Survey (USGS) were present for the workshop. This workshop was part of a multi-park scoping session also involving Petrified Forest National Park, Navajo National Monument, Sunset Crater National Monument, Wupatki National Monument, and Walnut Canyon National Monument.

The workshop involved a half-day scoping session to present overviews of the NPS Inventory and Monitoring (I&M) program, the Geologic Resources Division, and the on-going Geologic Resources Inventory (GRI). Round table discussions involving geologic issues for Pipe Spring National Monument included interpretation, natural resources, the status of geologic mapping efforts, sources of available data, geologic hazards, and action items generated from this meeting. A site visit was not made to PISP as part of this scoping meeting.

Currently, the greatest issue facing park resource management is dealing with the potential threats of resource loss from the springs drying up. Spring discharge rates have decreased from 60,000 gallons per day (gpd) during the 1960s to 15,000 gpd today. Tunnel Spring has captured the flow from Main Spring.

It is hoped that a new geologic investigation by the USGS at PISP will supply pertinent information on the geophysical nature of the spring system as well as produce much needed derivative geologic maps to aid in resource management at PISP.

Geologic Mapping

Preliminary geologic maps of the PISP area were done in the 1950s as part of crude reconnaissance mapping. The Short Creek NE, Fredonia NW, Short Creek SE, and Fredonia SW maps are preliminary at best and need significant refinement even though they are at 1:24,000 scale. The four quadrangles of interest to the park correlate to the existing photogeologic maps as follows:

Quadrangles of Interest	Existing Photogeologic Map
Moccasin	Short Creek NE
Kaibab	Fredonia NW
Pipe Valley	Short Creek SE
Pipe Spring	Fredonia SW

Dave Sharrow (PISP Hydrologist) and George Billingsley (USGS-Flagstaff, AZ) informed the scoping participants of an existing USGS initiative to conduct new geologic field studies that would involve mapping the entire extent of PISP at a 1:31,680 scale. This would cover the four quadrangles of interest to PISP. The proposal is outlined in PMIS as project number 61103 and is titled Geologic Mapping and Seismic Profile Investigations in Support of Geohydrology of Pipe Spring.

As part of this project, extensive geophysical studies would be completed to better understand the nature of the springs, faults and regional hydrologic picture. Margot Truini is the USGS lead for this project and George Billingsley will likely be doing much of the field mapping. Total cost is approximately $308,000 and has been funded by the NPS-NRPP as of November 2001.

Digital Geologic Map Coverage

At present, a digital coverage of the 1950s photogeologic maps is not known. In the event that digitized versions of the existing maps are not found, and until new larger scale mapping can be accomplished for the PISP area, participants suggested that the existing 1: 24,000 scale photogeologic maps be scanned, registered, rectified and digitized for use in a GIS. These can serve as a preliminary geologic map until new mapping is completed.

When new USGS mapping for the area is completed at 1:31,680 scale, a refined digital version will be part of the deliverables.

Miscellaneous Items of Interest

- There may be significant seismic hazards associated with the Sevier Fault because it runs through PISP; hopefully the new mapping will delineate any such issues and offer suggestions on how to recognize threats to park resources.

- The USGS has already published *Geohydrology of Pipe Spring National Monument Area, Northern Arizona*, by Margot Truini as Water Resources Investigation 98-4263.

- Current natural resource staff at PISP are Dave Sharrow and Andrea Bornemeyer.

Scoping Meeting Participants

Name	Affiliation	Position	Phone	E-mail
Sid Ash	NPS, PEFO		505-856-5852	Sidash@aol.com
Karen Beppler	NPS, PEFO		928-624-6228 ext.263	Karen_beppler@nps.gov
George Billingsley	USGS	Geologist	928-556-7198	Gbillingsley@usgs.gov
Debra Block	USGS		928-556-7138	Dblock@usgs.gov
James Charles	NPS, NAVA	Superintendent	928-672-2700	James_charles@nps.gov
Sue Clements	NPS, PEFO			Tecumseh@selway.umt.edu
Tim Connors	NPS, GRD	Geologist	303-969-2093	Tim_Connors@nps.gov
Helen Fairley	NPS, Flagstaff		928-526-1157	Helen_fairley@nps.gov
Tracey Felger	NPS, GRCA	GIS-specialist	520-556-7164	Tracey_felger@nps.gov
John Graham	CSU	Geologist	970-225-6333	rockdoc250@comcast.net
Susan Hanson	NPS, SUCR	GIP	520-526-0502 517-264-3944	Slhanson@adrian.edu
Kevin Harper	NPS, NAVA	Archeologist	520-672-2720	Kevin_harper@nps.gov
Ron Hiebert	NPS, NAU-CESU		520-523-0877	Ron.hiebert@nau.edu
Sherrie Landon	NAVA	Geologist	307-755-1336	Slandon@uwyo.edu
Allyson Mathis	NPS, GRCA	Interpreter	520-638-7955	Allyson_mathis@nps.gov
Todd Metzger	NPS, Flagstaff			Todd_Metzger@nps.gov
Michael Ort	Northern Arizona U.		928-523-9363	Michael.ort@nau.edu
Bill Parker	NPS, PEFO	Paleontologist		William_parker@nps.gov
John Rihs	NPS, GRCA	Hydrologist	520-638-7905	John_rihs@nps.gov
Dave Sharrow	NPS, PISP		435-644-4318	Dave_sharrow@nps.gov
Della Snyder	NPS, GRCA		928-226-0163	Della_snyder@nps.gov
Nicole Tancreto	NPS, Flagstaff		928-556-7466 ext. 240	Nicole_tancreto@nps.gov
Jessica Wellmeyer	USGS	Geologist	928-556-7267	Jwellmeyer@hotmail.com
Brenton White	NPS, NAVA		520-672-2720	Brenton_White@nps.gov
Paul Whitefield	NPS, Flagstaff	NR specialist	928-526-1157	Paul_whitefield@nps.gov

Pipe Spring National Monument
Geologic Resources Inventory Report

Natural Resource Report NPS/NRPC/GRD/NRR—2009/164

National Park Service
Director • Jonathan Jarvis

Natural Resource Stewardship and Science
Associate Director • Bert Frost

Natural Resource Program Center
The Natural Resource Program Center (NRPC) is the core of the NPS Natural Resource Stewardship and Science Directorate. The Center Director is located in Fort Collins, with staff located principally in Lakewood and Fort Collins, Colorado and in Washington, D.C. The NRPC has five divisions: Air Resources Division, Biological Resource Management Division, Environmental Quality Division, Geologic Resources Division, and Water Resources Division. NRPC also includes three offices: The Office of Education and Outreach, the Office of Inventory, Monitoring, and Evaluation, and Office of Natural Resource Information Systems. In addition, Natural Resource Web Management and Partnership Coordination are cross-cutting disciplines under the Center Director. The multidisciplinary staff of NRPC is dedicated to resolving park resource management challenges originating in and outside units of the National Park System.

Geologic Resources Division
Chief • Dave Steensen
Planning, Evaluation, and Permits Branch Chief • Carol McCoy
Geoscience and Restoration Branch Chief • Hal Pranger

Credits
Author • John Graham
Review • Dave Sharrow, George Billingsley, Bruce Heise
Editing • Steve Hoffman
Digital Map Production • Jim Chappell and Stephanie O'Meara
Map Layout Design • Josh Heise and Georgia Hybels

NPS 321/100624, January 2010

www.ingramcontent.com/pod-product-compliance
Lightning Source LLC
Chambersburg PA
CBHW080909290526
45795CB00007BA/2462